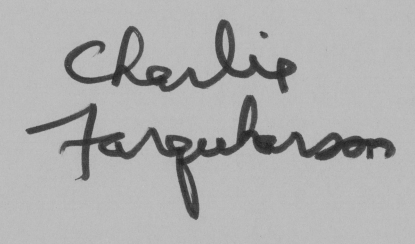

Cum Buy the
Farm

Cum Buy the Farm

by Don Harron
as told thru
Charlie Farquharson

Macmillan of Canada
A Division of Canada Publishing Corporation
Toronto, Ontario, Canada

Canadian Cataloguing in Publication Data
Harron, Don, date.
  Charlie Farquharson, cum buy the farm

ISBN 0-7715-9500-X

1. Farmers - Canada - Anecdotes, facetiae, satire,
etc. I. Title. II. Title: Cum buy the farm.

PS8565.A78C48 1987   630′.971   C87-094543-2
PR9199.3.H37C48 1987

Design: Peter Maher
Photo research: Hilary Forrest

Macmillan of Canada
A Division of Canada Publishing Corporation

PRINTED IN CANADA

*This book is respectfully
dedicated to the vanishing Canadian—
our "small" farmer*

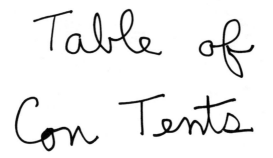

Table of Con Tents

Fore Werd

A close reedin of yer Gud Book shood make anybuddy think twicet about ternin over the soils fer a livin. Our first forepairnts got kickt out of yer Garden of Eatons fer gittin mix up with sum ferbiddin froot. Before they took a mind to snack offa yer Tree of Life and remane immoral ferever, God clang the park gate shut rite in ther face and rored: "Frum now on yer gonna homested outside on a few akers of wildernest! Yule both erns yer livin by the swetts of yer brow, and yer mane crop is gonna be thorns, thissles, and childern. Yuh wuz dirt to start with and that's how yer gonna end up. Now git sum close on and git to werk!"

They dug in and kep diggin, and the first thing they perduced wuz Cane, what cum up in 9 munth. No sooner had they started in fer to raze Cane, along cum Abel. Abel becum a sheepskeeper, and Cane a plowboy, and the speshully-ization of aggerculcher begun. Wen it cum to sackerfice time at the Sundy offrin, plowers cum off secund best to sheepers in God's Book. I don't wanna say yer Allmitey was perjudissed, but the saim blaim thing happen

1

to my Scotch incesters in yer Hy-lands too hunnert yeers ago.

The oney smart one in that first extend-it famly wuz No-uh. He got out of farmin fast and into yer boat-toor bizness, takin on bored cupples only. He wuz yer first sucksessful bizness ontryprenhoor on accounta he manage to flote a cumpny wile the rest of the world wuz in likwidation. After a 40-day note frum God, however, it wuz back to the land. Wen them passinjers land on Mount Arreroot, first thing they dun wuz spill ther seed in hopes of a harvist. First thing No-uh planted was a wineyard and perseeded to git drunk sittin bare-ass in his tent. He must hav had secund thots about wat it's like to be a farmer agin.

"Don't be a farmer." That's yer fore werd.

1.
Sines of Yer Times

I jist this minit finched puttin the FUR SAIL sine up, and my boy Orville has jist flashed me and Valeda with his browny. I never thot it wood cum to this. Valeda Drain Farquharson and I is bin in Holy Acrimony 35 yeer, and we is married to this soil jist as much as eech uther. We figgerd we'd both be leevin this place in a wite pine box. And not too far aways, neether, fur with both our wills we has ast to be inturd in lokel Muskoky dirt between the crevasses of our beluvved Canajun sheeld, witch we hav allways took fer granit. Now Ile probly end up in a ashtray in sum sitty creamertoryum, on accounta after we sells out, we won't have sex feata erth fer to call our own.

I mite jist have held on to our old fokes homested if Orville, the only issyuh of our martial union, had wanted to take up his father's hoe and hayrake, but he sez he don't want to liv the life of no crazy gammler, down on yer nees every nite prayin fer rane or shine, so he's heddin for the sitty.

The wife and former sweetart and I has bin awares fer kwite sum time that we has bin on the list of yer indangerd

3

speechies. Let's fase it, small farmers don't count fer a pincha coonshat in this land no mores. The price we is gittin fer our weet is lower than a preggerunt dackshound, and hardly nun of us is gittin by without bein subsiddyized by the guvmint. Sitty peeples cunsidders us a drane on the pubic purse. Even the guvmint is startin to say that mebby small farmers shud git outa farmin. Gon is the time wen Canda wuz yer wirld's bredbaskit. My gol, we're even outclass in this departmint by Chiner and Injure, and they're probly usin tools out of yer Stoned Age.

Well, this old sun uv toil is finely gittin out. I'm jist this side of three scores and five, witch meens that in a cuppla yeers I gits off on my Canda penchant plan. Farmers got no uther plans; weer the leest perteckted of all yer seenyer sittizens-to-be. We got no costa-keepin-up-livin clozzes, no sickleeve or workmen's condinsation, no extry hospitable or dentical plans haffpade by emploirs, no holdaze, jist 12-hour shiffs thout overtimes.

So with this federast jerryatrick handout I'm not exackly goin to my grate rewards, like yer sentaurs up ther in that Nashnul Mooseum of Parlymint in Ottawar, ware all the fossils is still breethin. (Valeda sez a sentaur is haff a man with the ass of a horse. You figger out witch end I'm tockin about.) I unnerstan the guvmint will give ya yer penchant erly if yer willin to be marked down to cleer out sooner. But I think Ile skip that haffprice bargin sail and hole out fer the full amount in 2 yeer, insted of all this demand-a-Tory premachoor derangemint. Meentimes I'm hopin to sell this farm so's the wife and I kin keep boddys and soles together till deth do it to our parts.

Sadisticly speekin, ther's oney 250 thou farmers left in the hole of this country. Mosta us is wat they calls marjinall, witch meens we ain't worth fussin with if yer bein gross about yer nashnul produck. The Wise man hoo minsters to us in aggerculcher keeps hintin we shud inroll in

4

Farmers reech the end of the rode. Full stop.

sum commyune collitch and lern sumthin elts to do. We are seen as bottom-rung supplyers and our bottoms is by now pritty well rung out.

Farms is treeted like any uther bizness today: if they don't perduce they git shet down like a wore-out goalmine. Big bizness is allways lookin fer them as kin git the goods to them cheeper; that's why they luvs to do deels with yer Farthesteast cuntries like Sous Kareer, Tie-one-on and Indeeamneezia. Farmers hopes fer prices that's stayble, but bizness speckelaters is hopin to git in on sum rabbid fluck-you-asians on yer bullish sockmarkit. They makes profits by byin cheep and sellin deer, and a wore or a faminn is a quick opperchewnity fer all that. Them birds got no intrust in ackshull fud produckshun, they spredd all ther fartylizer around on payper.

That's why big farmers is reely becummin mangers fer sum corprit aggry-biznessman, workin fer an absentease landlard hoo ackshully owns the farm as a invessmint, jist like sox'n'bonds. Mind you, it's the farmer, not the speck-

5

elater hoo takes the risks. Yer farmer is tole wat to grow and wat to spray it with by these corpulent jyants, and they sell him all his supplys, and buys, prosesses and markits the crop he sells them. But if he don't cum up with that sertin crop, or axsept ther prices, it's tit-sup time. This don't meen nuthin to yer consoomer. Fer them import fud is jist as good as any homegroan, even in seezin. We used to be self-defishunt in pares, plumbs, peeches and apeycots, but now import froot cums in before ours is pickt and drives our prices down.

Farmers reely feels like secund-class sittizens wen they goze to their banker. Bankers say they bend over backerds fer to help us, but they has most of us over a barl lookin the uther way. Yer bank slo-gun is "Wen you suckseed, we suckseeds", but if yer shite outa luck, they kin tell yuh to go suck a lemming. It ain't all yer banks falt. They're still smartin frum them dumm lones they maid to big cumpnys like yer Doom Peter-oleum and to hole cuntrys like Maxyco or Berzill. But it's hard to be rood to a hole country or even a malty-nashnul corpylation, so, jist like you kicks the cat wen yer wife yangs at yuh, banks took it out on ther lo-cal peeons, us farmers.

The old sayin is that banks will lone you thur umbreller any fine day and ast fer it back wen it ranes. My expeerients in our reesent reseshun is they'll lend ya jist enuff bin-dertwine fer ya to hang yerself. Sum farmers south of our parts got cricketsized fer takin invasive ackshun wen the banks fourclose on one of them. Wen they sent out a ockshuneer fer to sell off the cattles and chattles, he got a little more ockshun than he bargin fer. The farmers toogether bot all that partickler farmer's masheenery fer mebby ten sents apeece and then giv it all back to him.

I kin unnerstand sitty peeple gittin nervuss wen mild-manor farmers starts actin up like viggly-auntys, but to them farmers up agin the barnwall, they dint feel like ren-

6

nygaids. They jist put ther waggins in a sircel like them plutocraps duz wen one of ther nummer is up the crick, without a padding. They wuz jist doin sum in-cider tradin, witch is poplar mung yer up-aginst-the-Wall-Street boys.

If we hedda owed millyuns instedda thousands like Doom, or Messy Fergoosin, or billyuns like the Thurd of yer Wurld, mebby the banks wooda treet us with more respeck. Nacherly they cant afford to be charitabull accountance, and they sure got the wind up ther bankdrafts wen sum of us started to seam like Bony and Clide. But bankers aint at the mersey of yer elmints the way we is, and they wuz the ones wat cum on as the Lone Arranger wen they encurged us to expand our lands. If farmin in Canda gits up to anuther resessyun like '82, and the saim thing happens to yer intrust rapes, it may be yer sitty fokes' tern to be hit in the bredbaskit.

God nose we farmers is in the minnorty. You non-farmers is repryhensitiv of 95 preesent of the popillation of Canda. That meens almost all of our peeples has bin freed frum the so-call drudjry of razin yer own fud. To sitty peeple, the distribewshin of fud is sumthin that happins between yer

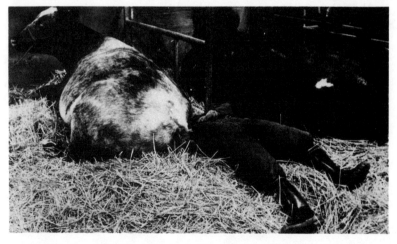

Farquharson completely cowd by the derry air.

7

soopymarkit and yer soor. Everythin is outa site and outa mind with yer flush toilit, but you mite be shock to lern that mosta the wirld still uses yuman waists in the Serch fer Excremence to flour ther feelds. Yet the cheef end produck of yer modren urbane life seems to be garbitch and pil-looshun.

All my life I bin a mix farmer, and its too late fer this old dog to tern a noo trick. But I got no proper livin, accorn to them sibilant serpents in Ottawa. My farm is listed in the Infernal Revenge-you as a hobby farm, witch puts it in the same cattygory as paintin on velvit or clectin stamps. I never went in fer this aggrybizness, witch is puttin all yer akers in one markit baskit, like the Wesstern fellas has had to do with weet, and now the guvmint is tryna set them on to rape. I hopes they kin all pass the fizzicle.

I've bin part grane, part derry, a little froot, the odd beef, and alwaze a chick er 2 on the side. With all that I shooda bin as happy as a hawg in heet. But the Milk Markuppin Bored squoze me at both ends, leevin me in the middel hol-din the bag; the ship disterbers on the Grate Lakes went against the grane; and my hens kep standin with ther backs to that Gorgin-Bay wind and layd the saim aig 6 or 7 time. I cant cut down ther ovaryhed, and with wat Bobloblaws gimmy fer a duzzen, it's not even worth cleenin them off.

Us farmers cant win. If we gits a bad crop we gits less munny, but if we cums up with a bumper, we still gits less munny. We are cot, as they say, on the horns of a dilly-enema. Our perfessyun has became wat the Good Book alwaze sed: "A Onner without Profit in our own Cuntry."

2.
Pie-in-Ear Daze

Us Parry Hooters has bin sellabating our Sintennyell all thru 1987. Us Farquharsons had bin round thees parts, tarin up the bush till they settle down, even before that. Our grate granpairnts wuz 69ers, wen the aria wuz first open up fer homestedding that yeer. As soon as they wuz bushed out, them Farquharson pie-in-ears found that the grounds they had burned away to start a farm wuz more like a sandy beech. Ther dint seem to be no place like loam.

Sum erly settlers, wen they hit ther sandy bottoms and found it wuz oney a cupple inches frum yer rock bottom, giv up farmin rite away and went lumberin off into the bush. After that farmers and them bushwackers wuz offen at lager-heds on accounta them lagers dint care much wat happen to farmers, not by a damsite.

If my fourbares had giv up stickin ther seed into the sand, they mite a dun better gittin ther rocks off in sum quarry. These are rocks of ages up to a billyun yeer, and we still finds the odd saw-tooth stone in our roty-tiller, witch wuz drop by sum Stoned Aged man mebby 7 thou yeer ago. He

9

Two of my fore bares (Parry Sound 69ers).

was tryna make a point with sum wildlife passin thru,
mebby poler bare or carrybooze heddin to and frum ther
articks, witch in them friggid times probly hung down as far
as Tundra Bay.

Histercal sooveneers is still croppin up round our parts.

A big brass bole was flushed out frum under a pinetree by one of our first inhibitants, a big sucker mebby 36 pound, and it had on it a flurry da lease, and the figgers 1636— probly the dait not the price. Sum antropoidollajist thinks it wuz a morter fer grindin corn and probly bean brung up to Middland by Jessywits wile they wuz porridgin ther canews up to yer Mortar's Shrine. It kin still be seen over to Trout Lake at Beaty's store, but it sposed to cum to its finyl rest soon in a West Parry Sound Musuleum fer pricey-less abjects.

Even before that, yer founderer of Cuebeck, Sham Plane cum by our parts and perseeded to drop his tool. It wuz a bit of brass call a asstrolabe wich fell outa his luggridge hard by Pambroke and wuzn't retreef till 3 hunnert yeer later by sum vally boy hoo wuz smarter than old Samplane, hoo didden seam to noe his asstrolabe frum a hole in the groun.

But nun of these visiters was reel setteldowners. Even the abridgeinall peeples treeted Muskoker as a kind of Nomad's Land fer to pass thru as quick as possybull. Ther wuz nuthin much groan abuv ground but sum blooburys, so yer passin savitch use our lo-cal as a kind of snackstop on ther way to summers elts. Nowadaze Parry Sound looks like most uther towns on this continence, thanks to them branched plants of frenchfrises that has sprung up everywhere—Mickdonald's, Burglar King, Kernel Kadaffy Frayed Chicken. Noware will ya see a sine "Home Cookin", cuz all our lo-cal burghers is out eaten them malty-nashnul burgurs. This makes everplace into a no place, and it's eezy to fergit ware you is if yer jist passin thru at snacktime.

Since the oney urbane dwellin Valeda and me cud probly afford is a apartmint, we cum down to Trontuh this spring fer to visit with a re-tire cupple hoo wuz now livin it up hy in a sluberb of Hawgtown called ScarredBurro. We pert neer had palpytashins tryna visit them on accounta they lived on yer thurty-furst flore and we didden noe about the exca-

11

vater, so we walk the hole way up and by the time we got ther, both our breths wuz cummin in short pants.

After supper I hadda git laid down fer a rest and wen I woke up our hostass wuz watchin the TV, and Valeda had disappeer. Last thing she had bin seen doin wuz watchin the lectric dishwarsher. It wuz pert neer midnite before we finely found her on one of yer umpteenth landings of that bildin, with a broom in her hand. Sints she cooden help with the dishes she had deeside that sweepin off the backsteps wood be the naberly thing to do.

One thing Ile miss wen we moove frum yer outbacks is not havin to wurry so much about munny even wen I got nun. Morn more peeple up heer these days is takin eech uther out in traid, witch is how we barters our bred, exchanging yer tats fer yer tits. We dun this a lot afore back in the thurtys, and speshully back in them fruntear daze ware ther wuznt much that was leagly tender. It's like the song writ by them Beetlebug boys: we gits by with a liddle help frum our frends. Farmers is still that way, and sitty peeples cood do worsen band together and help eech uther. Valeda sez that seenyery sittizens duz a lotta that, speshully them Wite Elfint Sails wher everbuddy brings sumthinthey got no use fer. Most wimmin brings along ther husbins.

Most of them seenyers livs in ittybitty boxes of apartmints, wellstacked on toppa eech other. This is wat is call "urbane renooal", but it looks more to me like packagin yer poor. If they gits too old fer partmint livin then they gits a rest home, but it ain't the kinda home ware you kin liv with yer privates. It's all kinda orgy-nized like a girls coedjycaishnul camp fer ocktoeginaryans.

If yiz want fine out how my incesters happen to end up in this parta the wirld, give a tern to yer page.

3.
The Berth of Faminism

Farquharson is a Gaylick word meenin "very deer one", probly deferrin to the cost of livin amung yer Hy Lands. Our slo-gun is rit on our scutchin in the old Roamin tung: "Fido et Forty-Chewdinhay." In the Anglican its "Fidel Itty and Fartytewd", witch cums out in Canajun to be "Hold on fer deerlife, Don't lose fathe!"

The Farquharsons manage to do all that up till a cuppla hundred yeer ago. We is deesent frum yer Thaina Fife, Mickduff, hoo wuz told to "Lay on" by eether Mac or Beth in that old Scotch play by yer Beerd frum Avon. But that was afore our famly got clobberd at Clodden by the English mercymarys, and our Bony Prints Charly hadda drag his way outa the country dress up like Flory Micdonald. Frum then on the Sassynacks took over, and them Anglish landlairds deeside that Scotland wuz inhibited by the rong thing—Scotsmin. They thot it wood be better to raze sheep instedda Scots, sints its possabull to skin a sheep morn once. It wuz downsize time, too. Fer to look after a hillfull of wooly lams, rams and youse, it oney takes won sheepmaster with won crook and a stout paira rubby boots.

13

Farquharson famly re-onion, 1929. Me in cap & cote, front row, and aint changed sints.

Rents went up quicker'n a gale farce sou'wester up a kilt, and thousands of lowly Hyland farmers were evictamized.

Yer common peeples tried to pertest, but all the uppity orders, like yer church, cheefs and Edinbuggers all mostly co-opulated with the Anglish innimy. One of the mane problems was that Scotland wuz becummin bilingamal. Yer hi Scot muckymuck was lernin yer Anglican, wile us low muckymux was confine to yer Gay Licks. Yer middlin classes wuz ankshuss to git in with ther Anglish Uppers, and thot of us poor soles of krofters as the arsend of Grate Brittens noo Empyre, sept that the sun never sets eyes on us, cuz it never stop rainin. Them Scots fezzants never had no rodes, bridges, or even britches to call ther own. They wuz parta yer thurd wurld, jist a 18-senchury Bangyerdesk. Nobuddy hadda taist of vennizen any more cuz ten sheep was now safely grazin ware the deer and yer mountin gote had plaid. Wurst of all, they went agin our grane, witch was the sorce of our gratest invenshun, Husky Wee Baw, yer watter of life. That's wisky to you Sassynackers, and all troo Scots feels they wuz led by the hand of yer Almitey by distilled watters til our cups runneth over with raw spearits that keep us Scots taped together.

My incesters wuz a buncha mix farmers in a modren age of speshully-ization and they wuz about to vanish in 1 big ewe-turn. This probly sooted the pasters in the churches cuz they found sheep to be less trubble than yuman beans wen they had to be shepperds over the lokel flock. Yer clurgy, yer foremen, and yer strawbosses pritty well all clobrated with yer Anglish oversneers in roundin up all the obsolene pezzants fer shippin overseize. And wen ther wernt no more underlings fer to be over, them same tackmen found that they too wuz outa a job and wuz in line fer to be export therselfs.

The rich had no trubbles sellin out ther country to the Sassynack furners. They jist got rid of ther dire estaits and hytale it into Ednaburg, where they lay about reedin them Wavy novels like *Ivan's Hole*, rit by Walt R. Scott, witch maid them all roomatic about a nevernever Scotland that oney axisted in frickshun. Even today they all kilt up once ayeer, stick a tammyshatner on ther heds and a jirk in ther sox, and pertend to be Hyland cheefs at a dinner-dants.

So wat happen to that feerce indypendint Scotch spearit, so long a terdition in our land? I'm not talkin bout yer Shivers Wreegle now. The one art of wore at witch Scotch cooden be beet wuz fightin with yer broad's sored. But that had becum a expork, as Berdish genrulls sent yung Scotsmen over to Yerp fer to fite agin that Boney Part. Many a slubaltern wood cum home on pashnit leev only to find his barns razed to the ground, and his buttin ben pole-axed by yer pole tax. It wuz a hint to ship up and let sheep in.

Sum refuse to go acrost yer Atlantical to be spacifick, and they wuz dump on yer coast oppsit them eyelands of yer He Brides fer to dredge up a bare livin harvestin the see by the gatherin of yer clams. It warnt till later that anybody spoke up about this farced exxodust. That low-lander (and sum say low-lifer too), the grate Scotch pote Raw B. Burns, wuz the first one with rime and reesons to rale agin the ritch landlards, but by that time mosta them evictimees wuz acrost the oshun on anuther continent.

A branch plant of our fokes had gon with the Erl of Sellchurch and wuz freezen ther behookeys off not far frum Winnypeg's Porridge and Mane. Uthers of our Farquharson cussins lit out fer Novy Kosher and they end up Antagonistickers, and they still feels that way today.

Our own partickler branch of the Farquharson famly didden wanna jump off to the ends of the erth jist yet, witch is wat they herd Canda to be. But the sheep wuz eetin our gardens and the Birdish soljers wuz arson around, so wen our cottedge wuz put to the torch we deeside to leeve before we maid ashes of arselfs. We didden hav enuff convickshun fer

16

to go to Oztrailyuh, but we had had relayshins in IRA-land, so my fourfathers set out fer Belly Fast, not reelizin how troo that name was to becum.

Wen the remnuts of our desprit famly got close to yer Emriled Aisle, they cood see them green green hills and figgerd the ground cuvver musta bin foreleef cloverd shamrocks. Terns out they wuz pertater plants, but that still sounded like goodluck to my stummick-extended famly. Tock about yer stable fud, spuds had bin brot to IRA-land frum yer Staits a cuppla senchurys before by Sir Water Rally. They had took so good they becum yer blooplait speshul 3 time a day fer all the lokels, mostly cuz the Anglish landlords (oh yes, they haddem over yer Ire-ish too), who was deporting all the weet and otes and barly, had a subsistint dyet. Them Irish sure fill up on taters, even if they wuz depraved of ther daly bred.

Our immygrunt Farquharsons wuz met at the ship by our rezdint cuzz-ins hoo asscarted them all the ways to Drum Horey, sumwares in yer County Dunny Gall. The Irish Farquharsons wuz even smaller farmers than yer Scotch brand. Ther hole spred wuz about the size of the sheep-pens ther Scots cussins had jist left, and all they groo on it wuz taters, witch wuz on the menyou every day. No meet, milk, or even the odd sangridge. And ther drinks wuz sumthin call Tay, witch wuz hot water with a spoon standin strait up. Mindyou, the men had sumthin out the back call Pot Sheen, and taken strait this home broo wood take the nots outa a barbwire fents.

Wen they wuzn't tendin ther crop—and taters don't take much tendin once you gits the bugs out—them Irish Farquharsons spent mosta ther time doin too thing: fitin and laffin. My Scotch Pressedbyteerian relltivs cooden figger wat ther cussins wuz allys fitin about, and sertny felt they had nuthin to laff about, sints they slept in a pigsty cheek by jowls with the pig.

17

Farmer waitin fer a rejisturd litter.

Wernt too long after the Scotch parts of our famly settle in and got the pig to moove over, that the bad times started. Them de-bugged pertaters got hit by the worst vire-us sints the Bloobonnit Plaig, infechshunatly noan as yer black deth. Watever it wuz, it tern the taters black, and it put the blite on almost as menny peeple. Histerians now say it nock off morn a millyun, cat-licks and ornjmen both, and sent anuther millyun and a haff fleen to Amerca. Most of them Irish immygrunts end up blow yer 49 parlell of lassitude, wher they got jobs as pleecemen in Newyorksitty, or as diggers, not of pertaters, but of yer Eerie Canall. Before this hollycost happen, yer Emmerold Ile had more popillation than yer States, but the rotten taters sure took care of that.

Watever had hit them spuds had cum frum the Staits in the first place, and the blite hit all over Yerp. But oney IRA-land had a big fam-in. But fam-in is man-maid. Ther's alwaze bin enuff fud in this world fer to feed everybuddy in it. IRA-land had lotsa fud to feed its starvin, but it wuz

18

export to Angland, on accounta them Irish had jist bin sined up in a freetrade deel. Lotsa nacheral reesorses goin out, and lotsa cheep goods comin in, that wuz the derangemint to revittle-ize IRA-land with all that forn devestmint cummin in frum yer Berdish, but it work jist the uther way. Three quarter of yer Irish crops wuz ship acrost Sane Gorge's Chanel, and all the profets wuz kep in Angland by them absentease landlards.

Sound familyer? Ther wuz a lotta stuff goin on back then sounds like the contemptuary mess we is in today. Yer Irish guvmint took a modren Canajun reproach to ther problim. They had 61 Parlamental commitys over the nex 30 yeer and a hunnert and 14 Roil Commisshun Reaports, every 1 of witch end up on the shelf jist like all ars do. Meentimes yer Old Sod becum the Ethymyopia of its day, with mornmore inhibitants livin on lessnless land under cultyvation. And the saim blaim wuz put on our lokel yokels as is put on yer Afferkan now. The Irish guvmint wuz realy Anglish, and they look down on ther undylings fer bein so randy and rutty that they were now long on kids and short on foodstuff. Sum ritch foke sed that mizzery had to run its corse cuz it wuz God's way of keepin' down the copulation explosion, and the oney uther slution wood be Sibble War—and them North Hibernyuns bin spearmintin with that ever sints.

It wuz this kinda IRAte altitude that maid us Farquharsons finely git out. By now, Canda sounded like yer Last Retort. The oney places left in Bellyfast fer desprit ruriels tryin to hole up in the big sitty wuz jails, loony bins and army barks. That wuz yer extant of guvmint housin in them good ole daze. (Sounds pritty much like her Metrapopolitan Tronto housin set-up rite now.) Ther wuz Farquharsons of all ages cum to Canda and ended up in ther qwaran-teens wen they land. But they wuz aloud in, witch mite not hav happen today, wen immigrunts is no excuse.

19

4.
I'm Wun Eara and Out Tuther

Small farmers is deffnilty outa stile. Our producks use to be the makins fer the rest of the country to git thru life three times a day, but most peeples tooday thinxs of fud as sumthin that cums not outa yer ground, but offa the shelfs of a soupymarkit. Most modren urbanes dont even have a frunt lon. I seen a cuppla sluburbinites watchin a truck go past with a lode a sods. One fella tern to the tuther and sed: "Wooden it be grate to hav enuff munny to send yer lon out to be cut!"

I reeds histry, and rites it too wen it's too wet to work, and I bin diggin into pre-histercal aggerculcher, witch seems to hav start back about 7 thou B.C. (witch stand fur Before Cunglomrits). Wen man grab aholt of his first tool it was fer the hunt. Fud to him wuz sum animal on the moove, so yer first tool wuz sumthin sharp to stick it with and arest its prograss. I dunno hoo got th'idee of stickin it to the soil insted, but it wuz as big as step as yer weel, yer steem injun, or even yer atomical bum. Makin the coneckshun between disterbin yer erth with a stick, and havin sumthin cum up munths later is a pretty sofisticated thot. I suspeck it wuz

20

Northurn Ontaryo Stoned Ager.

sum drunk hoo tride to make mush outa sum wild weet er barly, hated the taist, leff it to rot, and cum back weaks later wen it wuz bubblin. I bet them Stoned Agers got booz before they got bred.

Hoo drafted yer furst beest fer to help him dig up the tuff terf? Instedda fillin a bison fulla arrers, like it shows in them cave drawrins 20 thou yeer ago, it takes a mitey mind to stop huntin sumthin to the deth, tern around and git hitched with it to yer tool. First you has to taim the dam thing to do yer bid-in, then you has to tie it up and feed it regler so it'll be sum use fer the saim work tamorra. This is a lot more complickate than wildbury pickin.

21

It took skills fer to do all that, and it still duz. Even more than it takes fer to drive a trackter, cuz a trackter may hav more horse-power but its got no will-power. Masheens got no life after you shut them up, don't hav to be comed and curried, jist gassed and oiled and turn on and off.

Wen yer caved man giv up huntin fer groan fud he hadda stop wandrin round willys nillys and settel down in one spot, so's he cood keep his eye on sumthin that wooden run away, but wood grow bigger eech weak, and laider jist stand ther and let itself be plucked. Mebby yer first farmer wuz that drunk hoo felt dizzy frum that rotgut and wanted to becum lessonless mobeel and settled down fer the sake of his stummick. Or mebby the hole thing wuz a axident. Valeda thinks the father of all farmers wuz that Old Testymint fella Onan hoo dint reelize he wuz spillin his seed on the ground.

Wen man puts his seed in the ground, he hangs around permamint and afore you noe it up sprungs a sivillyization. First of these was nye unto the old Gardin of Eatin at the junkshun of yer Tigerass and yer U-fraidys rivers. Hstercly speekin, this is pritty much the saim spot whare them 2 kinds of Muslin, yer Sunny and yer Shee-ite, is still goin at eech other.

Yer Earakkers, woo is Sunny, keep tryna beet the Shee-ites frum out under yer Ayetoleyuh Cockamamie of Eye-ran. This is all happnin on the site of Pairadice, so mebbe the wirld will end ware it started, wat the Bibel calls Army Get On, yer last call. Them Earakkers alreddy made a U.S. open holy-in-one in yer Purrsian Golf. But let's get back to our begginings of sivllyization insted of brewding about the end of it all.

Not only wuz Eatin yer Nummer 1 Garden spot, but even after that wuz closed, and we hadda scratch fer arselfs, it staid the senter of things on account of its nice clime-it. Now it's mostly dessert. The hole aria was called Sumer, and it wuz too, all the time, so that a smart farmer cood have two, mebby three crops a yeer. They dun so good at farmin that twernt long before most everybuddy went frum barly livin to a hevvy sirpluss, witch they traided fer lintseed oyl with the Seeriacs, hoo wuz called back then Messdupatameyuns.

Wen you gits sirplusses ya gits traiders, and wen you gits traiders you gits markitplaces, and before long you got a sitty spreddin out frum it. Evenchly, yer sittys turns into a umpire, and by then most peeples is too busy deeklinin and fallin all over eech uther to bother about gittin in yer crops. That Roam 'n' Grease bunch wuz like that. Yer filler-sofical Geeks wuz too bizzy sittin down and jawin with Sockertees, oar studdyin Playdough.

Yer Roamin wuz too bizzy takin baths frum yer ackwy-ducks fer to git ther culcher frum aggra. Roamin meels cum frum a broad, as they spred thersels all over the noan wirld and exackt tribewts frum all ther subjeck peeples. They had the gaul to do the same thing to ther small farmers as them Anglican Saxyfones dun to us Scots. The feelds wuz givin over to sheep, and they dint bother to seprate the sheep frum the otes, so all them small farmers end up with wuz garnteed unemploymint lines in Roam. The rest of them Roamins lined up fer bred and sircusses, witch wuz put on at yer Colassalseemen, by yer Lion's Club, at the expanse of yer Christyun.

Meentimes that Eejipped bunch wuznt much better to ther help, altho they sure kep them off unemploymint. They kep draggin them poor fellahs outa the Nial at plantin time fer to work fer the Kyro Faro's Peeramid Club, strickly on the Cheops, with no workmen's constipation fer hermias from liftin them big rox.

Farmers has allus had to do extry bits on the side fer to git by. In ther Middel Ages, farmers wuz meer share-croppers gittin mebby ten purrsent of the gross producks of

23

sum Middle-evil barn or dook. They also hadda serve as mercymarys, and down tool and up crotchbow enny time ther lordenmaster yelled: "Serfs, up!"

No wunder they call this yer fewtle sistern. And nobuddy ever call them farmers; jist downrite villeins. This maid them pezzants sorta revoltin after a wile, but nuthin much cum of this infirmative ackshun, sept sum up-markit smerfs hoo got offa the land wen they found it wuz more muddel-class to moove to the sitty. You'd think that wood make urbane workers more speshulized, but versatilititty soon becum all the rage in yer next eara, witch wuz call yer Renny Sonce. Th'idee wuz that variety makes fer yer spicy life, and you shud hav the noe-how to do everythin. Sounds like small farmin, but all they dun wuz rite pomes, sing ballets, fite drools and ride bearback. Nowares do they ever menshun cleenin out a pigpen.

One thing them Renny Sonce Bornagenners dun wuz to uncover the Noo Wirld, witch is wat they call our parts in them olden daze. Evenchly they did speshalize in 2 trades, explorayshin and exploitayshin. Mind you they didden invent that, both had bin dun before. Even natifs had natif slaves of ther own long before the witeman cum along. Yuman beans has bin treeted as nacheral resorces since time in memoriam.

Aggerculcher wuz never consider one of Canda's nacheral resorces fer the longest time. In sum ways we is still strickly a firtraidin place, tho now it's more oil and compewkers. But the prinsipple is still the saim: explore fer to exploit. Looie Forteen of Frantz thunk of Canda as a buncha pelts of links, vermin and beever fer his mistrusses. Loozyanner wuz open up on accounta them sliver mines in Maxyco, not fer to settle peeple. Yer witeman cum heer oney to uproot or undymine sumthin he cood take back with him.

Wen the first Injun hand over his beever and got a

Nowadaze the yoke's on yer farmer.

mettlenife fer it, he reely went thru the changes. Frum then on it waz hard fer them Abridginalls not to think of the Bay, fer they deepended on that traider fer ther nex blaid. Same thing as happen to our Injun is happnin now to small farmers, as they try to sell us more masheens and tern our akers into strip mines.

Most of my famly's trubbles kin be laid back to yer Industyreerial Resolushun. All of a sudden, a facktry wuz hirin more peeples than farms ever did, and country peeple moved tord them to gane ther liverly-hoods. Now a facktry is a speshlized place, makin' jist wun thing in bulk to be deported all over the wirld. This is now happenin to farmin, and everybuddy is expeckted to be a speshulist on yer assembly line. The wun thing all of us got in common now is that everybuddy's end produck is the same: munny.

But it wuz yer Bull-shy Resolushun in Rusha that reely started to orgynize and soshulize her farmer. And it were start by sum Marxman frum Jermny hoo had never run a farm, but jist bummed round yer Berdish Musemun, makin tracks like yer Commonest Manyfisto, witch ast peeple to

25

join yer collectifs and throw off ther chanestores. This Marks wuz askin farmers to unown ther land, witch is the last thing they ever wants to do, but them Resolooshanarys all assoom farmers wood be tickelpink to becum Red soshulizers. Farmers is a indypendint bunch, and yer Roosian breed, called Koolaxe, wuzn't keen on all this Marxmanshit. The first leeder, after yer zar got blown away, was Vloodymeer Illitch Lemmin, and he had enuff sents to pull back on this socializing stuff, and let his peeple go to seed first.

But nex cum that old Jo Stallion, hoo wanted no truck with indyviddle farmers, and wen they pertested, he collectivized them all by shippin them off to yer freezones in Sybeerier. No farmer reely wants to work fer anuther boss, that's why Roosian aggerculcher has bin a freeasco, with the biggest black mark-up in the world. Ma'scow is the under-yer-counter capital of the wirld. The new fella Garbitchoff is tryna get rid of that no-insentiv sistern after all these yeers. Goodluck to him, but yer Chineese is alreddy way ahed. And why do you think ther's all the trubble among yer Fillupeenises? Cuz they got no steak in ther own soil, same with Senteral and Soused Amerka incloodin yer Salivadores, Watamalans and Nickerarguers.

Wat am I goin on about these forners fer, we got trubbles enuff heer at home! Aggerculcher in Canda today is a unmeddicated dissaster, but I like to think I'm a optometrist, not a pessaryist, so tern the page to find out how to do it rite.

5.
The Bertha yer Aggrybizness

The wun thing peeples cant seam to do thout nowadaze is munny. As yung tads reered durin our Deep Depressyun, we had no choist. But we had a cow, a hawg, a chick er too and we got along fare enuff. Not like in the sitties ware they hadda line up fer bred er soop, and this is happnin agin today.

But a famly farm wuz a self-contane liddle eunick that maid all of us in it self-defishunt. Nowadaze farmin is called Aggravibizness and yuh gotta be a speshulist to be part of it. God noes we gotta hav speshulists like docters or even bankers and liars, but we never had better meddlekill care took of us than by our old Jeepy, hoo noo all of us and our fokes frum berth, and spent haff his time sayin: "Don't ever do that dam fool thing agin." In our day that wuz preventiv meddlesin.

The speshulists in yer Aggrybizness is pritty well all frum universaltys. They is all trained to mine ther own partickler bizness and run around like won-ide munsters without bothrin to look over yer academickle fents at the uther fella's facultys. Oldtimer farmers like me is consider

27

by these peeple to be unskill workers cuz I don't fit into enny of ther neet cattygorys. Yer Aggry perfessers figger they're in charge of farmin like liars is in sole charge of laws, and fillosofers is in charge of morales and ethnics, wile they both leeve God to yer theeorylowjins.

Thanks to our aggerculcher speshulists, farms are now divide up into 2 kinds: them as takes hevvy ekwipmint and them as don't. That's why farms has got so big, cuz you need a lotta akers fer to justinfy poorchasing wun of them air-condishun combines with a glasscab feechurin yer AM and yer PM raddio with a steereo-foney Victorola attach.

Git bigger or git out, that's farmin today. Morn more small farms is gittin abandon into weed patches, wile the big ones is gittin ploud past ther fentsposts rite to the hi-way. I think this all start up in yer fiftys wen gaslean replace otes as the mane prime moover. So we sole off our horses and fed our otes to the cows cuz everybuddy in Northamerka wuz gittin into the backyard barby-queue, and the high steaks wuz in beef cattel. Weet becum a bit of a drag on the markit back then too, so we fed it to our beefs.

To farm big yuh has to borry munny and that's wen bankers, not yer aggryonomist, becums the speshulist in charge of us. If you heer sumbuddy describe as a farm experk, you kin bet yer gumboot he's not makin his livin as a farmer. Mebby a common-tater or bawd-caster, spoutin frases like "Aggrypower ginrates aggrydollers thru aggryexports". And they luvs to boast that thanks to yer hy-tex in Ammurrica oney 3 purrsent is feeding the uther 97 with morn enuff leffover to meat the markit demands of the resta the wirld. Well, that tiney minerority is so good at ther jobs in yer You Ass, Canda and yer Yerpeen Common Mark-up that the wirld is drownin in mountins of weet, milk, and aigs, wile them poor Thurd Wirlders cant afford to buy a thing frum us. They say the problim is distrybushun, but mebby its retrybushun fer all them bank lones.

28

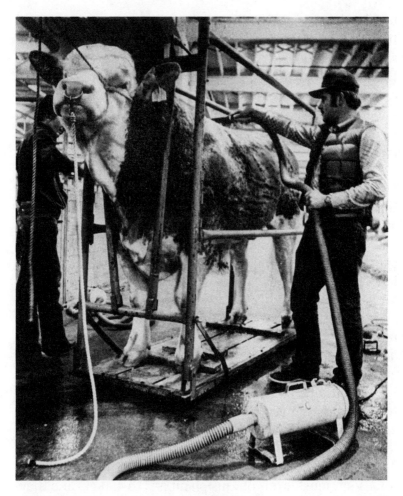

Modren farmin ends up in a vackyume.

I giv up my horses thirty yeer ago, and my Herferts 5 yeer ago, and went hevvy into weet. I dun good fer three of them yeers, but now it's the vicey of yer versy, and I'm sellin weet to my breeder nabers at bargin prices, cuz the oney beef I got is agin the guvmint.

Now if I'd staid in both biznesses I mite a cum out even, but I don't noe that I'm ever likely to git even agin. It's a littel like that tonick Valeda makes me take evry winter, Beef Iron and Wine; bilds you up as it tares you down, so that wat you lose on yer rustybouts you ganes on yer swingers. Bak in yer fortys we use to hav round our parts wat they called yer Beef Ring. It wuz kind of a co-hop of a few farmer nabers that kep us out of the butchershop, sints we took terns assastinatin 1 huge heffer or bullox every munth and passed the parts around prive-it.

Farmers allwaze mange to co-opulate in tuff times. Nobody in yer thurtys seem to own a combine or even a thrasher. We all gang up together and rent one in consert, and then we'd all gang-thrash eech other. Yer farmer has bin a genrullist hoo noo a liddle bit about everybuddy eltses speshulty, but our mane speshulty wuz takin care of the land. This is not wat farmin is about today. Yer speshulist farmer has tern into a exploiter hoo likes to git into the land and git out fast—a wambam-thankye mam. But a reel farmer noes he kin deepend on the land oney if the land kin deepend on him. We are not jist extrackters; we are nurcherers.

Modren aggrybizness trys to tern farmers into facktry werkers hoo happen to liv in the country, but not nessessarly close to ware they works. Jist punch in and out, and leeve the controlls to a absentease landlard hoo cood be a big malty-nashnul corpulation. The thurd wirld has not yet folla soot, most farms on this planit is 3 to 4 akers and they still diversifys ther crops. But in Canda yer small farm is sloely goin the way of yer buffloe. Sept that *them* beggers is thrivin with reservayshins, mostly in nashnulized parks. If Sassakat-chewon wuz put to grass, them farmers wood make more munny cleenin up on yer bison. They cud fatten them up with all that weet. Lets hope they don't speshully-ize like them wite hunters dun a hunderd yeer ago, takin out the tung and leevin the uther 2 tun of carcase fer to rot on the planes. They're doin the same now huntin poler

30

bares with a helluvacopper and oney takin the rug part home.

Environly-Mentalism is in the papers every day now. Our first inhibitants wuz practissin all that before we land on them. In fack it was ther relijun. The Injuns didden think of yer invyronmint as seprit, but as spearit. And they was all part of it, no more ner less than anythin else on yer Muther's Erth, and they all had a persnal relayshunship with that big Muther. Accorn to yer Redman relijun, Her and Them is in a constant whirl of goin thru the changes. All of us, plants and aminals, passes thru eech other and out the tother side. We is part of whatever sirrounds us, so that nobuddy ever feels aloan, long as ther fulla erth spearits. We cant jist liv by and for arselfs and eggnore our Muthers Naycher, fer she is a too-way street. Yule notiss that sitties is gittin to hav morn more 1 way streets.

But we solvd our natif problim by pennin them up and teechin them to fowl ther own nest. And we suds-siddyize this squaller like a crop we don't wanta grow no more. Peeple fergit that Injuns wuz our first farmers. Yer Eeryquoits wuz groan corn in the middel of Trontuh 12 hundert yeer ago, and even then they had a better plitickle sistern than we got now. Now they're backd into corners fite-in fer ther rites to look after therselfs in the old waze before pro-grass overtuck them.

So our first famlys has bin kick into the corner of histry. But ther is a bunch follyin the saim kinda beleefs, putting yer eckollogy over yer teckology. I'm tockin bout yer Aimish, yer Hutaright, and I dunno how menny Mennanite. They is the best peeple at restrainin therselfs I ever see. You probly seen them as you wiz by them in yer car. Both of youse is goin to markit: yer in a helva hurry to stock up before the hoarders gits ther, but these fokes is jist a clip-cloppin along in a horse with a buggy behind. You'd think they wuz all goin to a funerall the pace they is goin and the

Menanite cattel bires lookin fer sum auction.

close they is ware-in. Or cherch, mebby. Funny enuff, they ain't got no cherch. They hold servisses regler, but it's in ther homes or even ther barns. And ther's no minster lordin it over them by degrees. Their preecher is chose by lottry,if they ever use sich a word. And nobody gits paid fer doin any of that. Them tellyvishun vangelists must think these pee-ples is stark stare-in nuts.

But these peeple got the saim altitude to Naycher as our Ab-originals. You gotta giv back to Muther Erth wat you took. Modren aggerculcherists hoo is outstandin in ther feelds say leeve it to the experks to figger out, speshully if they is in the hire of a kemikle cumpny. Wile ther all erjin farmers to git morn more expansive, these Aimishable pee-ple gits morn more restrainin. And modrens sorta snickers at them as sum old-time relick, like a scarecrow. But the point of tillin yer erth is helth. Not jist fer yerself and yer land, but yer hole commoonity, yer land and yer planit. And yer Mennanite bunch has dun this by restricktin therselfs in every way, frum masheens, frum wore (they are all patsy-fists) and, as much as they kin, frum guvmint—federast, pervinshul and moony-pissiple.

Everybuddy elts thinks these peeple is kwaint, pitcheresk, weerd, exstream, backerd, probly slubversiv, and certny over-relijuss. But any farmer hoo noes his salt, noes that they're the best at ther job of any of us. With small farms fallin on all sides, these so-call relijuss fan-nyticks kin take them over and expand, but not into a meggy-bizness. They is self-contaners, pervidin ther own wellfair, secyourity and sociabull insurience, by ignorin guvmints with ther undivide attenshun and stickin to ther own famly and common-unity.

Wat's ther secreet? They don't compeats with one anuther! They don't use all ther no-how fer to pray on eech uther, and they don't cast-off ther old peeples or bandon ther childern. Summa ther childern is leevin the farms, but that's cuz this bunch is so blaim furtle that sum of the yung has to make ther way in the towns, cummin back on weak ends fer all that home-cookin that makes yer lips shmeck together. Fer them that staze, everybuddy is bizzy and every-buddy has a use. And wat we mite call demeenin drud-jery they calls Good Helth-keepin fer the sake of awl.

They wood say that the werd perduckshun is a dillusion of yer mail eego, witch thinks it duz things all by itself, and is out to brake all reckerds. But reaperduckshun needs yer femail part too, and this act happens not once, like in a stripmine, but agin and agin, seizin after seizin. I got a dis-taff on my staff and I'd abin bankrupchured long ago if she hadden bin round fer to keep our books and me outa the porehouse.

I'll tell you ther uther secreets. Wile the rest of us farm-ers is sayin "Let us spray", they're out rowtatin ther crops every yeer frum rye to weet to corn to clover and First and Second Timothy. That givs them bugs no chants to settle down and raze a famly over the winter, and also lets yer goodlady bug do her work fer free. These Mennanite noe that erthworms duz more good than trackters in yer long runs, fer them little burrowers brakes up yer soil, and makes it eezier to work. Them trackters compacks the ground like a horse don't. And horses gives you less erozeshun not to menshun instant-on the spot-deliverd fertlyizer.

Mebby we shud all take lessins frum these Cristchun farmers. We all got eclectic lites but sumhow I think we're more in the dark. Speekin of witch we pert neer cum close to freezin in the dark a duzzen or so yeers ago wen the Arbs had us over a barl, but we restraned ourselfs and becum oily conservayshunists so that now them sheek peeple is up to ther barenooses in glutz of oil. Mind you, the same short-edge cood happin agin if we don't take a kew frum our best farmers, yer Aimish, woo ar a lotless Aimlesh then the rest of us.

6.
Unpoplar
Meckanix

I mind the time back in the thurtys we got our first lectric lite bulb. I wuz litterly in shock frum the blaim thing. I cooden mange to tern it off, I tryd blowin it out, and finely I hadda cut it down with my scoutnife. Never in all my life felt so much hell cum outa 1 peesa twine. But gas has giv me the most trubble. The infernal cumbustyawun injin has rool our lives sints I wuz abel to crawl on all floors. And the masheens that housed them injins is now litterin our countryside, rustin in peece at the mersy of yer elmints.

We has a standbye car in our orcherd. We call it standbye cuz the blaim thing don't go. It wuz a 1958 Edd-sell, and we use it as a roost fer sum chicks hoo don't git along with the uther hens in ther house. They tell me yer Edd-sell is now a anteek. It wuz a freeasco wen it wuz new, but now they say I cood git good munny fer it if I put the weels back on, git them chickins out and give it a spray job. But I think them foul haz awreddy beet me to it.

Masheens kin be left out in the cold, but peeple are more complecks, counterdickery, all-round unpredickabull and a

35

helluva lot more fun. But pert neer anybuddy has got more soshul statues today than the fella works with his hands manyally. Nobuddy wants to work up to be a master kraftsmen today; they'd druther be soopervisin mangers and ware a tie. The hole idee is to move up and on, not stay whare yiz are to becum better at wat yer doin. But yer hand laberer thees days is maid to feel like he's jist this side of kittylitter.

Mebby we shud start restraning masheens, insted of retraning farmers to do sumthin elts. Masheens make haist, but you noe the old sayin, "Haist makes waist." That must ecksplane why Valeda, whoose allys runnin around, has kep her gurlish figger.

Twenny yeer ago, mebbe thurty, we all herd of the cummin revvylushun in aggerculcher. Peeple dont like the idea of revvylushin applyed to pollyticks but its accceppabull if yer tyin it to jist froots and veggibles. It meens distrybewshun is so good that we can hav strawburrys in Jannyerry and termaters all yeer round. Mosta the crop is pick by poplar mechanix and they even grows them squair so they'll fit better into them little cartins. The fack that they taist like 3-ply dont seem to matter.

Now I mind that they're tockin about a new meens of food preservashun called irradyashun. It seems its got it all beet over Valeda's way of preservin by jist puttin the stuff in them Free Mason jars.

All of us has bin waitin' sints 45 fer sum one fer to giv us that irradyated finger, but after last yeer's blow-up at Sharenobilge in yer Uke Rain, most of us is startin to think that it ain't yer wore-time uses of nukuler power that's got us all scairt, but yer peeceable ones. I mind wen the first muskroom clowd boom over yer Noo Maxycan Dessert even before they drop it on Heerosheeny and Naggasockeye, yer fewcherists was perdictin that them atomical bums wood be tern to peeceful piles and bring us cheep power frum all

36

Valeda becums a sax objeck.

that urinanium so's we wooden hav to bother with ornery
ways of gittin our electrocution. Batterys was not inclooded
in the yeers ahed, fer the rods and the staff of them
reacshunarys wood take keer of everything.

Well sir, it may hav bin cheeper power at yer start, but
the repare bills is startin to cum in, not in millyuns, Billy,
but billyuns, as our futility bills gits hire and hire. But
that's the leest of yer wurst. Nobuddy noes the trubble
they've seen round lotsa them atomickal piles. The oney
reezin we ever found out about Sharenobilge wuz wen it
crost all them boarders into Scandalnavya. The Serviets
finely cum cleen wen ther new hed Garbitchev bring in a
noo policy call "Glassnuts" witch is Roosian fer leedin with
yer chin.

They had jist as big a dust-up back in '57 witch nobuddy
herd about til one of ther sighentifficks defecated to yer
West in '76. Place call Kishtim in Scarbeeria had a buncha
plutonemeum waists go up in mushroom smoke. Now the

place is probly call Kishtimoff cuz the hole place, and wen I say hole I means it litterly, is uninibited fer hundreds of kill-yermeeters. Oh, ther's stuff growin alrite, clusters of grate big mushrooms. Must be God's joke fer to remind all them peeple hoo aint ther any more.

Mind you, the Yanks wuz pert neer as secreetiv about that neer-pattymelt-down they had at Three Pile Iland. This happen 2 weak after a moovy call yer "Chiner Sindome" with Jane Fondler cum out preevyouin the hole thing. It wernt about sum Shankhigh house of ill-repuke at all, but it sure call the shots on a buncha cows gittin ther tits lit up in peeceful medders hard by Harseburg in Pencilvaney. Everybuddy started to evaccinate therselfs as fur away as they cud git wen they seen the steem comin offa them piles at that radioactive plant. Up to that time we'd oney herd about that stuff happnin in yer Nevadder flats or them nuthin atolls in yer Souse Specifick.

We hadda line-up fer to see that Sinderdrome moovy, and the reezin wuz wen we got inside nobuddy wuz willin to sit neerer than 30 roes frum the frunt.

7.
Syints Frickshun

Everybuddy tocks about yer fewcher but so far nobuddy's ever bin ther, sept mebby thru the pages of Syints Frickshun, or mebby watchin Shurly Micklane on the TV, sept that she manely gose back into yer pastyers. Frum the way our farm experks and prognosstiffikaters spouts you'd think they'd alreddy bin ther, cuz they keep tellin us about the farm of yer fewcher: granefeelds ten mile acrost, derry cattel pend up in 7-story hi-rize apartmints, all overseed by a bubbel-doam controll tower with a compewker tickin out wether retorts and sockmarkit quota-tayshins, at the same time as it is runnin a remoat cuntroll roty-tiller-combine. As it glides acrost that 10 mile weetfeeld, the grane it is thrashin gose strait to the sitty by sum noomatick toob, and at the same time as its cuttin the weet and flailin yer kernel, this same masheen is peeparing the soil undyneeth fer the next crop.

Acrost the rode, beef cattel is fed enteravenusly by more toobs in anuther hi-condom-minimum wile anuther toob flushes all ther waists into Oblivia. At the saim time a packin plant is prosessin yer finishbeef into uther toobs fer shipmint. Overhed a hellacopper is sprayin insectinsides and herbysides, wile a lit-up plastical tararyum 3 feelds wide is bizzy shootin up ornjs, orkids, keewee froots, and uther unstabled fuds.

This rig is sposed to be a compleat inclosed sistern like the sirculation of yer blud. Run off frum uther plants supplies the farm with trickle-down eerygation. Saim deel with the cattel. The carbum dideoxhide frum the breths of them cows will be piped out fer use by the crops, wile the oxengin frum them plants will be pipe back fer use by the live stocks.

As yer orgasmic farmer mite say, this is pewr hunnert purrsent bullshit. Tote-all yuman control over naycher is as impossibull as it ever wuz. All it takes is a garbitch strike fer to prove that. And I think yer averidge titsmouse has more control over how he gits thru Janyerry and Fibyoufairy than sum square termater under that plastickal cuvver.

Planners stick to the fewcher cuz it's eezier. It hasn't happin yet, so they cant be call to a count. Scares me, that dubble vizzyun of wat's to cum. That hole opyrayshin I jist describe is run by 2 telly-farmers with a compewker and a redfone. No other layin on of hands. Sounds to me like them 2 soljers deep in that bunker in Coloradder sumwares waitin to see hoos tern it is to giv the finger to that atomical butt-on.

Nobuddy talks more about yer fewcher than aggravacul-cherists. It's more important to them than yer pasture, altho mind you, ya has to watch yer step in both places. And obsolenity is the order of the day. A masheen is ment to be use, and use up fast, so's we buy sum more. Us farmers has bin sold the fewcher 1 implymint at a time. The more masheens orgynize yer day, the less orderly yer life seems to bee, cuz we're becumming dependint on the competents of

40

a lotta anal-lists and pro-grammars who woodnt noe how to ficks a masheen to save their lifes.

The masheen's reckliss promiss of a reduckshun of man-power fer autymatick horsepower has depopillated our farms. Everybuddy tocks now about yer fifth genration compewter that thinks fer itself. I hav always assoom they are tockin about me, sints us Farquharsons has bin heer a hunnert and fifty yeers, and I computes into Tronto every weak fer to sell the wife's aigs. But I bin findin out that a computer ain't sumbuddy drives all the way into the sitty fer to make a livin. It's a electric-tonic masheen with a extended mammary and chips fer brains.

Sailsman tride to sell me one of these rigs the day I wuz diggin a fresh hole fer our skeptical tank. Fella leened over the fents to watch me, and kep talkin up these fantsy laber-savers, yer Burros, yer Honeywell and yer Eye B.M. He flapped his ruby lips in the breeze so long that I wuz finched diggin the skeptic tank hole before he got dun spoutin. I terned and sed, "All the wiles you bin yackin, I hav ackshully burroed a honeywell fer to take care of mye B.M." He still went on talkin about more moddles he got in his truck. I finely thru him offa the farm after he offerd to show me his Wang.

Now we're about to faze arselfs rite outa existints with roeboats. I don't meen yer sit-down punt with a pare of ores on the side. I'm talkin about compewkers with laigs, little tin men like Arsy DeeToo or SeeThru Peepio frum yer Scarwars moovy.

Ther makin cars now pritty well untouch by yuman hand. That new Toyola Coronary plant down in Came-britches Ontaryo is ternin out, of all things, Shevvy Novas with Toyola injuns. Wat kinda ads they gonna run on yer TV? "See the Ewe Ass Eh in yer Toyolet!" Nex thing ya noe Fords'll be ternin out Fordswagens with yer Owdy peeple that puts so many compewkers in ther cars they're havin totel recall. Or yer Jermin and yer Nipplenees will git together and spon a horde uv Japanees Beetles.

But this is yer presents and the fewcher remanes unoan and wun pursons's gess is as inane as anuthers. Take them hi-flyin intelleckshuls that gather together ten yeer ago fer to be yer Clubba Roam. They perdickted that by now we wood hav no oils fer to grees our weels and that we wud be in dire strates with our fud perduckshun. Hunger is still our mane produck, but meenwiles we is wallerin in sirplusses.

If you want me to gaze at yer cristleballs I cood say the famly farm will be histry by the yeer 2 thou, cuz farm incums in Canda has drop by pert neer haff, and land prices by morn that. Farmers is now gittin returns of 10 dollar a aker, and at that rape, yood hav to have 2 thou akers fer to stay abuv yer charty line. We all noe wat the fewcher reely is: it's the time wen them pollytishuns solvs all our problims fer us.

The wun reel thing about yer fewcher is that we is allwaze gittin sprized by it. Hoo wooda thunk a buncha green munkys foolin around in senterall Afficker wood hav spon a plaig that makes the hole wirld think twicet before munkyin around therselfs. Wat I keep wundrin is hoo started munkyin with them munkys in the first place?

8.
Cummin to Our Sensus

If yer wunderin wen peeple are gonna cum to their sensus, Canda dun this in 1986. They sent a buncha bizzybodys all round the country, nockin on yer dore and astin you yer age and sex at the time of your last berfdy. Fer sex I jist ansered "Infreeqwint", and they ast me back if that wuz 1 word or 2.

The reesults has finely cum out, and yuh mite be took back by sum of the figgers, like there bean a millyun Canajuns over 75 and that Baby Boomers haz tern out to be Baby Busters sen it cums to havin childern. Mane fack is that Canajuns is older than the last time they cums to ther sensus, but hoo cooden figger that out. Wat didden sprize me wuz the sadisticks fer us farmers. Back in yer thurtys 30 purrsent of us lived and worked on farms, and today, as I tole you, its lesson 5%. And yet it's became a twenny billyun doller bizness if you incloods holesails, retales, and prossassessing. That is one qwater of our grossed-out nashnul incum, and one tenth of our exporks. And tho our farm popillation is dwindle by two-thurds in fifty yeer, our akeredge is about the same. Most farms is bigger, and most farmers bitter. Most farms is in Ontaryio but Sask. and Alta. ain't much beehind. Noofunland got the leest, only 384 yewnicks, but they mostly goze in fer yer Mureen life. Watever they duz they seems to hav a good time. I becum a honorarium Noofinladder at yer Carryvan in Tronto by kissin a codpeece. If that's there idee of fourplay, ther welcum to it.

Speekin of witch, the breth controll habits is offal illoominate-in. Did you noe sevenny-too purrsent of Canajuns is on the pill, and 68 purrsent of them is wimmen? Sixteen purrsent is offen on it and twelf purrsent is offen off, ten purrsent is on it on and off, and 8 purrsent is off it off and on, but 7 purrsent is off it and wisht they wuz still on, wile six purrsent is still on it and gits off so selldum it don't reely matter. Fore purrsent say they don't know, and 3 purrsent say they don't care, but 28 purrsent say "No! Don't", witch shorta crossin yer laigs is still the most affecktif kinda berth control.

But lets lookit yer briteside. Child morality is cut in haff since 1950, and brest-feedin is back in stile with more noo Canajuns on the tit than ever befor. And last yeer ingagemints outnumber vasextummys, so the old fashion way of tyin the not is cummin back. It use to be that to be engage wuz almost as good as bein married, but a lotta yung fokes today thinks its even better. Multipple ingagemints is poplar too, witch substytoots a kinda soashibull poligmy fer leagle monotony.

I'm kinda sprize that ingagemints is in fer a upturn cuz the sackermint of marge is on a deafknit downtern. Divorse is 1 of the groath industrys of our fewcher. I mind wen the oney grounds fer gittin split in this land of ours wuz insannity. The wife and former sweetart sez it's still the cheef grounds fer gittin married.

A corse the cheef coz a divorse is gittin married in the firsplace. Accorn to yer laidist sensus, 2 marges in 5 in

44

Canda now ends up in yer deevorce cort, the uther 3 appairntly is deetermin to fite it out to yer bitter end. A lotta cupples deeside to slip outa yer holey dedlock wen this no-falt idee cum in. It's the saim idee they're tryna bring up in Ontaryo with yer Otto Insurience. If you ding sumbuddy's hart, or even jist bend it, yer not gonna git called on it. Jist let bygons be begon, you don't need no collusion after yer collision.

Duz that means that liesinces fer to git into Holy Acrimony is gonna hav a ex-piery date jist like at yer Burro of Ottoveehickles? Mebby ther'll be a lil coopon on the bottom of yer purrmitt witch you tares off wenever yer warnty or yer payshints runs out. In that case the oney differnts between a huntin and a marge lysince is that the ladder is took out after the hunt is over. I'm not too sure wether the split-ups cums frum missunderstandins or becuz both partys understands eech uther all too well.

Sadisticly speekin, divornce has shot up 500 purrsents in

Ever say Di, Charlie!

45

Canda sints 1968. That wuz the yeer Premiere Terdo sed the guvmint cant do its bizness in the middel of yer bedroom. That wuz the start of yer Mee ginration. But mebby now them baby bloomers of yer Mee ginration is ternin into a Wee Wee bunch, the way ther havin bloomin babys of thur own.

Th'idee of man and woman splittin assunder wen God hath pit them together goze back 5 thou yeers to yer Impire of BabyLawn wen King Nabbakidnister first seen the handritin on his outerhouse wall. The Babylawn words sed "Many Many Tickle a Parson", witch ment don't be in a hurry to hitch up or you'll split yer britchin fore long. Yer Roamun dun a lot of deeklinin and fallin out, too but divorcemints dyed down a bit under yer Christyuns, hoo put that stuff in the marge contrack about forslakin' all udders till deth do you apart.

Yer split industry was down in last yeer's sensus. Yer effluent sassiety peeples kin afford to split up wen yer pore has to still huddel in ther masses together fer to keep warm. The rait of brake-up is about haff in yer ruriel parts wat it is in yer sitties. Peeple on farms gits to noe each others falts pritty well. Sitty peeple don't call them falts. Ther marge cowsellers tells them its ther idiot-sinkerseas. There's no trile marges in the country, cuz ther's no sich thing as a trile child, altho every child is a trile in sum way, but that goze with yer terrortory. I think if it wuz as hard to git married as its eezy to git divorce, it'd be alot eezier on the kids. Pre-marge brakedown don't coz neer so menny complickayshines.

I went thru that back in 1492—sorry I musta got confuse with then nites of Clumbuss—I ment 1942 wen I wuz station at Camp Boredom, standin on gard fer thee and me so Hitler's Nasty Panzy divishuns wooden evade us. Or wuz she 45 wen it happen? By swinjer I wuz ingage both times, fer I cooden afford no dymond frum yer Berks, so I went to

46

the Wool Wurth and found this nice liddle pin with two flags on it with bloonwite stones. I dunno wat they wer, they look sorta like Smartease. Its the kinda semmyfor flags them navels uses and Valeda wuz tickle pink with it, but she ast me wat the massage of them flags wuz. Now I noo wen them sailers wiggywag at eech uther they're tryna say sumthin in yer Morris coad, but I didden noe wat it ment, so I rit back to Valeda that it jist ment I luv youse in flagtock. Well, my yet-to-be-wife wuz more preesistint than I wuz and went to the Parrysound Lieberry with her pin, and look up semmyfore flags in a book call "Jane's Fite-in Ships", and Jane musta toler wat them flags wuz saying to eech uther, cuz it deelay my ingagemint fer anuther 3 yeers. The massadge red: "Purrmissyun to lay alongside and cum abored."

The wife and I has relayshins in Coldwater (and bleeve me it aint all that much fun), but wen we visited them this winter they took us to a seeminar and disgustin groop at yer Oro Sex Clinick, called "Sex in the Erly 90's". Wen we got ther we cood hardly git in the hall cuz it wuz fill to overflowin with seenery sittizens. I never seen so many oldtimers at a pubic lecher, and they took a kind of jerryhatrick pole that nite, and frum wat they sed, seenyer sittizens (witch the wife and f.s. and Ile be in no time) seems to divide up into 2 groops. Them as never thinks about sex atall, and them as never thinks about anythin elts.

But the funny thing is yer furst groop is farfar bigger than yer secund, witch reely mounted to a cupple of dirty ole men in yer nimpymaniack minerority. Sex in yer resthome is not about to reeplace yer eclectric blankit. Most of our older elders is far too bizzy with ther hobbys, eether nittin on ther mackramy, or scatterin ther rugs. So insted of finding yer Over 90's atween yer sheats, yer morn likely to cum upon them all weevin in the halls or hookin in ther rooms.

47

Our punk Orville with anuther skind rat.

So wat about the onley issyuh of our martail yewnion, our boy Orville? Well, he looks to me like yer averedge haredresser but he seems to be a pritty devout hetterosectional, spendin mosta his time at this gurlfrends down the rode. Mind you, he plans to lit out fer Trontuh in single harness as soon as our hyscool boys and girls matrickulates together this Joon. The oney thing that boy is intrusted in is rottenroll mewsick, fast cars, and good rodes that'll take him as far away frum his ruts as fast as he kin make it outa here. Even if he wanted to stay on the farm, witch bleeve me he don't, we cooden afford to keep him at our traid. Besides farmin ain't a trade—sept mebby a free trade the prices we're gittin—it's more like a pashin. A pashin fer stayin put, witch makes me kinda a throwback to my fourfathers hoo wuz drug kickin and cursin frum ther incestral homes. And jist like them aneshint displeased persons back in 18 senchry Scotland, us modren Farquharsons is bein forsepsbly remoove frum our hairytage. Not by soljers this time, but by reelestait speckelaters, workin fer malted nashnul corpulayshins. Even farmers hoo is furfur biggern us is startin to git driv out by them big finanshul tyfoons.

So heer I am, a backwerdwoodsman, a sad remnut, waitin fer a deevorce frum my land. If it's no-falt, then I spose it meens never having to say yer sorry, but I am. Hooever moves in, won't do nuthing to keep up the land, jist hire sum infeerior desecrater to pritty up the house. Nobuddy is a settler any more morn a few weakends a yeer. The oney time ya heers the word settlemint these days is wen the deevorce deecrees cums out in the papers.

It's a bitter pill I'm takin. We spend the last twenny yeers teechin our yung peeple to be free frum worry about fertillity. Now we're gonna cap it all off by makin them safe frum worry by becumming a condom nation. I'm about to give that same berthcontroll pill to my akers of arble land, condemmin it to be a reckremational waistland fer sum sitty squire, hool keep my feelds fallo forever.

9.
Urbanes
vs.
Ruriels

Country peeple is not oney married to each other but to ther land, and they expeck the hole affair to last long after they've gon to the big Resthome in the Sky. But nowadaze it seems that country and sitty are exchanging inhibitants. Old farmers is force to move into small apartmints, and yung sitty peeple is tryna buy fresh air with less smug in it, and they'll put up with all that weak-end traffick fer to git it, inhalen carpin mon-oxhide all the way bumper to bumper fer to do it.

Yer uproot farmer meentimes ends up as anuther mygrant to yer urbane get-toes. It's yer Deekline of yer Roaming Impire all over agin. In the Staits, innersittys like Deetroit and Yewston are abandummed by yer Yuppy rite after five o'clock, leevin it free fer yer Poopy (yer Poorly Off Older Person). To be in stile today you mussin liv ware you works. Mumandad livin abuv yer Conveenient store is jist fer South Kareenin immygrunts hoo is willin to stay up 24 hour fer to git ahed fer ther kids.

Valeda wants to git a place neer one of them big shoppin malls like yer Eatin Senter or that Gurrmazian place out in

Edmington. She don't wanta fite the wether wen she's shoppin, and them malls is a kinda greenhouse fer peeple. Says Valeda: "Bless the mall." They got all them shoppers by the malls round our parts. The crowd on enny weak-end is like our church on Eestersundy, pack to the gilts.

I wuz feelin kinda sorry fer myself sittin wate-in fer the wife and f.s. fer to rap up the shoppin wen I run into a terbacker farmer frum down Dell-High way. Talk about never heerin nuthin but scurgin words, them fellers is gittin it all. Mind, I don't blaim the guvmints fer tryna cut down on yer lung lung trail awindin down life, but why keep pilin taxes on terbacka and make munny offa the avails of deeceese? Why not stop it all together and declair the stuff illeagle like yer hishash, and yer marruhjewahyena? Then all them terbacker farmers will probly make a fartune.

Mebby insted tho, they shood git outa backy plants and into rubber plants, fer that seems to be the new groath industree now that drugstores are selling con-dumbs by the gross. I never reelized how wise my old muther wuz every spring wen a yung man terns fantsy, she used to yell at me on my way to scool, "Charles! Don't fergit yer rubbers!" Everybuddy is intrusted in consoomer perteckshun packagin these daze.

Yer mall is becummin yer soashul senter of its commoonity. It's yer town squair without no wether affecks. A lotta farm cupples is startin to move into town even wen they still holds on to ther farm, cuz to keep up the ole place, they has to take a part-time job in town. And its not jist round our parts this is happenin. Practickly every small farmer in the country is sum kind of part-timer, incloodin the wife hoo has becum a ding-dong of a lady callin Ayvon all over our consesshuns to make the spair change she cant frum her aigs not gittin laid.

I keep thinkin bout our farm bein bot up by sum sitty man hoo oney cums heer on his vocashun and lets the land

51

go back to the bushleegs. Naycher all by itself is a regler tangol. It needs man's help fer to unsort itself. The forst is always waitin fer to run over yer feelds agin, and a good farmer is proodint enuff to teech feeld and forst to liv with eech uther. Sitty landlards thinks they is conservin ther land by lettin it go to rackinroon. Furst thing they duz is put a sine "No Traspissing!" Us lokels has a old terdishun of free traspiss and everybuddy unnerstands it. Frinstants, wun of our nabers is a big Trontuh corpulent liar hoo oney gits up to his farm a cuppla weaks a year. So we go on this absenteasers land every fall and gits the froot offa his appel-treese before they fallen rot. Fer us the sin is not in crossin over his barby-wired fents but in lettin them russits go to waist.

But a lotta plutocrappy hobby farmers is too ritch to bother about the froots of country laber. And they gits so upset wen sum pore workin stiff with a meany-ill job in Parry Sound, sets up a permamint traler on seemint blox and livs ther all-yeer round in full vue of thayr pitcher winda. This intyfears with wat Mr. Sitty Uppity sees, on accounta it ain't all that pitcheresk. Peeple on hollydaze likes to avoid realty. They want yer Grate Outdores to look like a paintin by one of yer Grooper Seven paint-by-number-ers, and they're used to switchin the chanel on the culler televishun wen they don't like wat they see.

But life ain't jist tellyvishun or moovys, as Runall Ragin started to find out this yeer, wen he wuz found in the arms of yer Ayetoleyuh Cockamamy, to pay off yer Nikerrogwan Contraries. Up to that time he had bin the most poplar prec-edent sints George Warshintun, hoo cood never tell a lie, unlike Tricky Nixon hoo cood never tell the trooth, and Runny Ragin hoo cant seem to tell the differnce. Run's problem seems to be lotsa aff-ability and not enuff respons-ability. But we shooden be too hard on a man has had his prostatate actin up at the same time as he has bin suffrin

The Old Shi-ite hisself.

frum the Aides he got down in his basement. They seem to of bin down ther takin the fifth, and singing "Old akwaintance shood be fergot and never brot to trile." On the contra, say I.

I bleeve it was yer Martial McClueman hoo sed that the TV has tern our wirld into a Glow-Ball Villedge. That's why Runny luvs to git on the TV, and that's why he's so good at bein yer M.C. of yer U.S. But reedin off a tellypromper aint the same as bein Precedent all the time. Runny has consyntrate on the first 2 letters of that word Precedent.

Eech wun of us has to be direckly responsibull fer sum small corner ware we are, and to briten it, if possbull. The Erth is all us yumans got in common, and that shud make us want to take keer of it. That old Chinee fillasofa Confuseyez sed that the guvmint of yer state is rutted in famly order. The Universable is jist as self-contane as yer famly farm, everythin hast to relayt to everything elts, or the thing won't run propper.

You take this Pay Equaltitty stuff. Valeda don't hold with bein eekwals with my sex, becuz she feels it wood be a turble step down fer her. She is the Canceler of the Exchecker in our house in charge of our strong box, and don't you fergit it. She givs me my allowants regler. I've sed it before and Ile say it agin: I wooden mind havin in this country of ours a nice prime mistress. The oney reesin I voted fer Briney Bullroney wuz becuz of his Yugo-slobbrin wife Milly. Why wood I vote fer a man coodn't even make a profet outa running a orehouse in Cuebeck?

I tole you Valeda aint no Wimmens Librium, and she's not lookin fer anybuddy to up her conshishness. She gits totely peeved off watchin Wimmens Movemints and she ain't intrusted in jinin' up with yer Letzbean Muthers or yer Gay Divorcys. When I ast her how she felt about capital's punishmint she sez if peeple wants to liv in Ottawa that's ther lookout. Wen I tole her it jist ment decrinimalizin the deth peanulty, she sed them Rite-to-Lifers feels it's not rite to kill anyun till after they're born. I ast her if she wuz a member of yer Morl Monopoly or one of them REEL wimmin hoo is tryna git Federast fund-in. She glare me rite in the eye, tole me she was no wimmin but a Lady, and don't you fergit it. She also tole me to stop thinkin about all this, fer a Open Mind, she sez, is the Devil's workshop.

10.
Gittin Rid of Nukuler Waist

Canda has alwaze bin big on yer famly. Speshully in big bizness. I jist red that this hole country of ars is run by six famlys, jist like in the old daze wen Uppity Canda wuz hitch to yer Famly's Compackt. Us farmers riz up agin them under Willie the Lion Mickenzy but we got run down by that Compackt pritty fast. And we got less chants of beetin the compact famlys witch is in charge now.

Witch is a shame, reely, cuz farmers is the reel risky takers, the troo entryprenhoors of this land, not them fly-by-nite capitolists with ther paper corpulashuns. Them suckers don't grow nuthin but fat on the profets of flippin papers and cumpnys backinforth, and sellin shares with no votes attach witch givs no power to yer peeple. Is that why us unwelthies pays all the welth tax, and let them tyfoons sit back on ther assets countin ther ill-got ganes, and excaping the estait tacks even wen they pass over to the grate Tacks Haven in the sky?

Lemmy hit yuh with a sadistic: 374 of Canda's biggest cumpnys is control by oney 1 duminant shareholder. I'd luv

Lord Tom's son shows the hole in his soul.

to noe hoo this fella is becuz if I cood do the layin on of hands on him I wood reed to him frum the Gudbook, Isayuh Chapper Five, vorse Ate: "Woe to those hoo add house to house, and join feeld to feeld until everywhere belongs to them, and they are the sole inhibitants of the land."

I tole yuh the big password theez daze is Compytishun. The reesin I am bean put to pastyer (but not to stud!) is cuz

I cant compeat with yer aggrybizness farmers. Aggrypower is mezzure by 1 thing, a markitabull sirpluss. Strickly fiscal attrackshun. Farmin is now more than jist a way of life, it's a bizness, so shape up er shit outaluck. But wen sumbuddy gits bigger, sumbuddy smaller is bein driv out.

But them big biznesss boys in that famly compack ain't intrusted in compeetin with eech uther, nowaze. They'd rather co-opulate as they sit on eech uther's boreds. That's not compytishun, that's Monopply and them suckers is on yer Bored Wocks and Parkplace wile I cant even pass GO. And yer big farmer with his big masheens is more deependent than me. He has to perteck all that investmunt and balants his books, as perduckshun overides his main-tenants. The man has had to tern hisself into a masheen that's consumptiv.

But all we heer in guvmint handouts is "Be compettytiv!" It wuz compytishun tween sheep and men, and taters and bred that druv my old peeple outa Scot- and Ire-Lands. Sumtimes "compytishun" and "prograss" sounds to me more like "munnopoly." I mind we had a Prograss Club back in Parry Sound in yer durty thurtys wen the only pot wuz on the stove, the only grass wuz on the lawn, and if yuh had inflayshin ya seen yer dockter about it. We wuz all in yer Deep Depreshyun at the time and after a wile the meetins of yer Prograss Club dride up cuz we dint see any. The guvmint finely thot up sumthin to cure us of our Depressyun. It wuz World War Too.

Now its Hy Tex-Nickelollogy that's gonna be yer pannaseeya, and everybuddy is rushin to bring out new masheens without trubblin atall about its effex on the workers has to use them. Like them Viddlyo Interminabls that's sposed to be a mennis and givin preggerunt wimmen funny babys.

And wat about all the dyed-oxen in the water? And them goddam PCB's? (not to be confews with yer Tory SOB's).

All them chemiccle deterrents in Ontaryo cums frum yer
Hookers up yer Lover Canal. Sitty peeple is startin to drink
ther water frum bottles. Valeda sez she noo them urbane
peeple drank but she never dremt it'd be jist plane water.
And they don't seem to reelize all that tocksick stuff they
put on their ittly bitty gardens kills a lotta uther things
besides bugs. I thinks the way they lays it on they shood
hesitaits to choo on a blaida grass. Meself, I'd druther hav
sum of them jirms around me than any of them pizens
they're sprayin em with. They'd do better puttin sum of ther
garbitch on ther gardins. At leest you kin bild soil with that.

The wife and I has His and Hers piles of rotten old stuff.
Hers is called composst and contanes anythin that'll giv life
to her gardin by rottin itself to deth. Tee bags, old lettuses,
old letters, carrit tops, sawed-dust, straw, twigs, hedgy clip-
ins, and domestical garbitch all gits together and cooks
over a long long time. Yuh cant buy stuff like that, ya has to
make it herself, and practickly anybuddy kin do it hoo has
jist had lunch. It pervides a nice place fer them mike-robes
to liv breeth and eet. And in winter I spred all my old spoil
hay to bed down the wife's cold frame fer to keep her in
heet.

Hoo needs pestysides wen we sulfer enuff with yer assy
drane? That may sound like sumthin' happens to yer stummick but it gits ye in the laiks first. If tooryism is gonna be
our Nummer 1 hevvy industery, then this stuff is gotta be
our Nummer 1 Pubic Enemma.

Mind you all that stuff ain't drop only by yer Yank. Our
Stinco and Smelco has maid ther own mark in this feeld,
and wat about our Ontaryo Hydra, hoo keep importin hy-
sulferin cole frum yer States instedda givin the bizness to
low-sulferin Elberta and the Marmtides. Things go better
with ther coke.

Runny Ragin has promiss a cuppla billyun doller but he
took the saim pledge last yeer fer to rejuice assydrane and
58

never sine no checks. He still sez he wants to keep on ivesti-goratin wher it cums frum, in case they are hevvy Repubel-ickan states. Cuppla yeers ago he sed it cum frum ducks, geese, and trees. He sed if you seen one redwood tree ya seen them all, and if he keeps on with this altitood he may be rite wen yer redwood becums yer dedwood and yer poor duckin geese is lyin cleer at the bottom of yer lake, wile we all sing, "Wat's it all about? Algy!"

Ackshully about 75% of yer assid dropt on us cums frum the Staits and about 25% frum ours. Works kinda like yer Otto-pack. Subbery, gaitway to Parry Sound, and the rock capitol of the wirld, brings up most of our nockterminal emissyuns.

Ther is a limit, ya noe. You kin look up on a stary nite and see the infinititty of yer Universal and think, "My gol, the thing don't have a end", but it duz, and it may be soonern ya thinks. Keep yer feat parrlil to the ground and remembers ya livs on Erth and it kin oney be use so far with-out gittin use dup. If you takes frum the soil ya gotta giv back. Works fine with plants and aminals. No waist ther. Yer magits is our best garbitch clecters, and reely cleans up. It's a grate set-up and has work fer millyuns of yeers. But man cums along and brakes all the rools, speshully sints 1945 wen he went nukelyer.

Now weer reely tockin about infinty and immorality. Them atomical waists we leev lyin around are gonna go on tickin fer neons of yeers. The Bibel sez the Lord giveth, but hoo will taketh away wen weer finched with it? Hoo wants a messa ploo-tone-meum wen our reackshunarys is all dun with it? Everybuddy agrees we shud git rid of the blinkin stuff, but wen it cums our way we shudders to think, and refuses the refuze.

That must be the theem song of this enda the senchury: Not in my Backyard, Buster. This is happenin even wen cot-tedgers move neer us in Muskokey and raze a big stink about the nacheral odor of pigs we hav bin livin with sints berth. Worst thing kin happen to a sitty house is to hav a biffy on the bum. But they don't mind spreddin ther own offal around wen they're fur afeeld.

We had a buncha tooryists camp side our hardwood bush one aftynoon and had therselfs a picnick. They dint ask, and we dint bother them, but Valeda, bein one of yer erly voyeurs, watch them thru the binockulers she uses fer the trots. (They're them racinhorses with sulky behinds.) Seein the garbitch they spred all over our place and left, she tuck down ther liesints number, and check up ther adress with yer Veehickle Branch plant in Tronto. Middel of the nex weak we druv down to sell our aigs and also to dump all that saim garbitch back on them sitty peeple's lawn.

But we gotta do sumthin about this nukuler garbitch, I tole Valeda, or we'll all be in the glowming oh my darlin. The States is ankshuss to expork summa ther bundels of ultry violents up heer. I noe yer not plannin to stick around that much, but this Plutone stuff is rettry-o-activ fer the nex 24 thou yeers wen it goes on to haff strenth fer the nex 24 thou. And we got 400 of them hotrods frum yer Pickerin Terdbines soakin in a noocleer bath, not to menshun about 150 millyun metrick tuns of peeces of tailing of radio-meum lyin round Elyot's Lake. Yer Federast pogrom fer to git rid of them wound down lass spring and now its up to yer pro-vinshuls fer to leed us down ther gardian path. That's gonna be tuff with ten premeers shoutin at eech other: "Not in My Back Forty, Shorty!" Mebby they'll stay up all nite shoutin at eech uther and tern the perseedins into a Sun of a Meech Lake.

Seems the oney thing that kin hide this mennis is wat's bin under my 2 inchesa topsoil fer dunky's yeers, or mebby I shood say fer dinashore's yeers. I'm talkin bout the shist of yer Grate Canajun Sheeld witch goze down deep to yer Molsen larva at the senter of yer erth. That's wher them radium-activ rods is gonna git a deesent berry-all.

Valeda thinks a erthquake cood still be yer big shist disturber. We never had 1 yet in Parrysound but we hav relayshins in yer Middleast—not them Lesbians on the Bay Route—I meen Noo Brunsick. Five yeer ago they had three erthquake in 1 weak. Sum yung cussins of ours got married the same time and holed up fer ther honeymoon in yer Hy Holyday Inn hard by Bucktoosh. They never leff ther hotel room the hole weak but they sware they felt the erth moove morn once.

These erupshuns started up ten yeer ago amung yer Peekynees. Mousey Tung wuz gittin reddy to go to his forchin cookys in the sky, so he call in his wife, Miz Tung, hoo's maidin name wuz Ying Yang or Yank Ying, sumthin like that. You mite a saw her a few yeers ago yackin away on the TV. They finely put her in the hooscow cuz she wooden shut up about the Grate Step Forerd, so they march her a Grate Step Backerd into yer clinck.

But that's all water under her bridgewurk. At the time weer talkin about, Mousey giv her his last willin testymint. "After I go, Yang er Ying, I wancha to giv this job to Dung Chow Ping." Then Mousey wuz a gonner over yer Gratewall of No Reeterns. But Mizziz Tung didden happen to dig Dung, so after Mousey went up, she flung Dung out, cuz she wanted nuthin but Wang Hung When. Now I dunno When, and I don't spose you duz eether, but the fella that finely got the job wuz Wack Yer Fang. Wacky becum Nummer 1, and Dung, like allwaze, wuz Nummer 2. I dunno wat happen to Wacky, but Dung work his way into yer top posishun and in cum sum noo fella on hoom it all depends, Hoo Yo Bang. He got in trubble last Chrismuss with the revoltin Universly Stoogents at Peeking U. I dunno hoo got Hoo but his place wuz took by anuther one had worked his way in, Lousy Wang. But that's forners affares.

Wat matters is that these Chinese eerupshuns spred all

acrost yer Gloab. The next yeer ther wuz anuther big wun over the back of yer Turky, and then ther wuz another down in the bottom of yer Chilly. (I usually gits an erupshun after a bole of that stuff.) Then ther was Ittly, Algereeria, Hy-wayuh, and then ther wuz the openin of that 2-holer in Warshinton Stait still spits a bitta dandruff over Vancoover. But the big 1 down ther is yet to cum, and they say it's yer Sint Andree asses falt, but my god, yuh cant blaim everythin on yer Cathlick church.

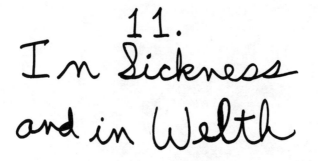

11.
In Sickness and in Welth

We all got a divesteed intrust in helth, of arselfs, ar land, and ar planit til weer stonedcole up the pipe, non-decompost mentalis. But the big trubble is that the fellas in charge of our helth, dockters, is more intrusted in dizeeze. And dizeeze is catchin. Sum of ther payshints starts to injoy ill-helth even morn the prospeck of gittin cured like a well-hung beef.

The wife and former you-noe-wat has became partly diabolick, and has to be shot reglerly with 1 of them hypodermis needel until she is filled fulla insolents. She also needs a few courtesans fer her arthuritis, and last munth after a consert fer yer Sick and Tired of yer Yewnited Church she stud up fer our nashnul antrum and sat strait down on her nittin needels. After this reer-end collusion she hadda go to the hospitabull and hav stitches remoove. And fer 2 weak she wuz lyin in bed under the doctor's soopervisor without a stitch.

Now she tells me she's got the cellerlite. I'm not tockin about sum dim bulb in the basement or yer rutseller. This stuff is jist a fantsy wird fer fat. And ther's a eppydemick of

Partissatrackshun: He shooda tryd tutchin his knees without bendin the flore.

it every yeer leedin up to Noo Yeer's Eve. I call it yer Calorie Stampeed. After Noo Yeer's cums the rezzolution, and dieyet is all wimmin tock about frum then on till after Lent is spent. They're all tryna git back to the scoolhouse figgers they had wen they was addled-lessints. Now it don't make no mind to me if ther's butter on the beams, I still warship the ground that shakes under her. But matoor wimmin is determin to starv therselfs so's they kin look like the scared crows that moddles fer Harpy's Brazeer and Vague. And they pays gud munny fer to go to a Ladys Diminishin Saloon fer to shake off ther choice cuts, with all the connipshuns they do on the contrapshuns that duz it to them.

And in tweentimes ther wate goze up and down like a

hore's drores. And if they falls offa the waggin then they'll all git together in hords called Fatguts Yewnannimuss and fladjellyate ther gilts wile they cricketsize eech uthers figgers in the nicest way. Left on ther own, without the mewchewell hatered of ther best frends, they'd bloon up into a Cooky Munster by Dumb Minions Day.

You shud see the cottedge-cheesy lifestile I has to go thru wen all this is goin on. This way fer to loose wate by eetin less and anorexersizin more seems to be the plan the Federast guvmint has fer us farmers. I think they're usin us as the thin edgy of yer wedgy fer to keep off the return of inflayshin (that's yewconomic tock fer blowin up like a bloon filld with nuthin but hot air). But ther don't seam to be much of a chants of any of yer Common Housers goin on a reel dyet, not wile they got that Parlmentally Restrunt that oney charges haff prices. We hav 1 haff of a wirld that cant help starvin, wile the tuther haff cant help goin on dyets.

The hole objeck of farmin is helth, and that incloods yer soil, plants, and aminals. It's a compleet sistern like the hole planit is sposed to be if we don't drives it to rackinroon. They don't seem to studdy up jogfree in school no more, and even histry is rejuiced to sumthin call "Soashabull Studees" or "Men in Sassiety" that makes eddication sound like a whinin'cheesy party. But joggerfree is wat we started with, and histry is the shite-offal mess we has maid out of it.

Sitty peeples has a peekyoulyer idee of helth. I bet ther idee of the Gudlife is to win the lottery, liv in lucksury and idolness and at the saim time be skinny as a rake. If you reeds that Plowboy maggotzeen put out by Huge Heffer, you'd think the prime objeck in life is to *be* a rake. After tarin up the town and paintin it red with the tango tribe of tenderloin nite-riders, they gits up in the mornin and goze to a jim fer to work up a swett on sum kinda fantsy masheen that don't perjuice nuthin but over-develop mussels and

65

tore liggymints. Or these yung urbanes'll git out and run several blox in ther undywares fer to work up sum artyfishul perspiration. And do you think any of them is intrusted in any kind of manyull laber like helpin the wife and I git in the hay? Oh nosirree, that's beneeth ther digglety. After the jim or the joggin they goze back to ther liddle compartmints and has a cole shower and brisky rubdown with a ruff towl till they feels Rosy all over. Then they turns on a buncha laber savin deevices that runs everthin fer them with a crook of ther littelfinger. And if they slip a cog wile axersizing, so that 1 of ther parts don't mash with ther uthers, they'll probly applys fer Workmin's Condimnation.

I red a artickle in last munth's Breeder's Diejest about yer Holy-istick Medsin. It's noo fangle, but it sounds to me its the saim kinda treetmint we use to git frum our ole famly dockter, or genial pracktishunner as he became to be called. Wat he wuz is yer non-speshulist. And we never went to his clinck, he allus cum to the house. He preeformed a applydicktummy on me and the charge wuz ten doller, but my father wanted my tonsills and adannoyeds out too so that wuz a extry $2.50. By the time they cleared me off and had him stay fer supper he oney charged us the ten.

Our docter noo all of us persnally enuff to tell wen we wuz fakin it. A lot of peeples do that to stranger dockters jist so they kin git the use of their meddlycares. That's why so manny peeples is takin playseebos, witch is pritty much like the fether they giv that Waltdizzly elfint Drumbo, fer to teech him to fly with his eers. Our old jeepy's treetmint fer foney ailmints wuz to giv you a good 1 up alongside yer hed. That wuz all the perventiv medsin we needid. I mind tellin him one time that I thot I was developin a trick nee. He tole me to jine the sircuss.

I've allwaze thot farmin and medsin had a lot in common.

66

They both sets out to be lodgicle and sinetiffick, but to make it work they has to ends up as a art. The soil and the farmer is like a dockter and his payshint, hole-istickly rap up in a intymit relayshinship. And farmers has to have their bedside manors wen they're tendin ther crops. Wen we had horses to plow instedda horespower, we hadda be a kind of sick-eye-a-tryst too, cuz beests work better if you sings to them instedda swares at them. And if you cooden sing, ya cude alwaze wissle.

"All one bawdy we" sez the old Him, and don't you fergit it, cuz wat afflicks yer hand sooner or later hits yuh in the brane. As a yung lad I allus hoped to be a Vetnairy Aryan, mostly cuz I was so shy, and ther payshints never tocks back to them. But I'm afrade the only 1 round our farm that's gradewated with degrees is my cow's thurmometer. But to be one of them beest dockters I wooda had to go down to yer Gwelf Aggravaculcherd Collitch fer to take a corse in Aminal Huzbandry, but my father had awreddy fired our hired man fer trying the saim blaim thing in the barn. (Axidently speekin I bin mitey lucky. Farmed morn 35 yeers and never had 1 axident yit. Oh, I've bin throwed by a hores, and kick by a cow, and bit by a snake, but I wooden call them axydents, them buggers dun it on purpuss.)

So I never did git the chants fer to take yer Oaf of Hippo-crisy like them Obstinit-patrishuns and Gineycollogists (witch to me is jist a cuppla fantsy wirds fer delivery boys and reparemen). Mind you I spens a lotta time dockterin up the wife. Every winter she catches sum kind of bug, not the kind you kin squarsh with yer boot, but the kind of back-teeria duz the inside job. So I goze downto yer Rectal drug-store, and this time I seen this stuff "No More Coffs, No More Colds" cost oney $1.69 so I brung it home and got haff the bottle down the wife before I red the dees-truckshuns that you wuz sposed to cote it on the bottoms of her galloshes, fer to keep her feets dry.

The hospiddle jist called and they want her in Mundy fer a test fer shuger, and noe-in Valeda she'll probly be up all weak-end studdyin fer it. She's bin pretty leary about hospiddles ever sints that Extry-Billy-achin strike they had last yeer. But I tell her that all them nurses is registerd consheenshus injecters with on-the-jab trainin and they will needel her proper with ther sick-shooters. But it's not the nursys and dockters she's worried about, it's the shortedge of beds. They got a noo cattygory now called yer semeye-private bed, ware they takes sumbuddy with a hy feever and puts 'em in bed with sumbuddy as has dubble pomonia, figgerin I spose that they mite cansel eech uther out. But Valeda thinks if you puts 2 strangers in the same bed it won't be long before the 1 is chargin the tuther user fees.

And wat cums after that? Pay bed-pans? Drop in a quarter before anythin elts? Nex thing yule see is a ad fer a short-order sturgeons that kin handel 4 tables at the saim time, or mebby a drive-in mergentsy wing ware yuh kin do it to yerself as you trespans yer own skull. We need that sort of thing like a hole in the hed. But them experks kin make misteaks too. I stud in front of 1 of them flooeyscopes and they tole me it showed I had a hole in my hart. So they took my pitcher with my shirt off in frunta 1 of them X-Rated camras and wen they look at my bonyparts ther wuz nuthing rong with my ticker. It's jist that I had bein standin in frunt of that folleyscope with a life-saver in my shirtpockit.

And then I got in trubble takin the rong pills. Insted of yer pencilinen, I wuz takin the pills the wife got fer her sweepees in the garden. Valeda sed I had bin swallyin yer eekwivalence of 800 pounds of sheep fertlyizer. I fone up the docter but I cooden git him, and his deesepshunist tole me to take 2 assburns and call her in the mornin. She dint say wat I wuz sposed to call her but I was sittin up all nite anyways so I had lotsa time to think.

I dunno wat to say about all them soshibull diseases that is so fashunabull now. Before yer Ades, it wuz Herpees the luv bug, and before that yer gunnerear. I mind the time a cuppla our Airfarce fellas frum round our parts took a Bomming and Gunnery corse over to Bellfast and wen they tride to picks up the lokel girls they never got to ther first base, becuz in Northern Ireland gunnery is consider to be a soshabull diseeze.

Mind you, weer better off than yer averidge Yank. Ther hospiddle beds is jist a park taxee with the meeters runnin. Cost you morn a hundert doller a day to stay ther, and I bet it's even more if you stays overnite. They're startin' to tock about Jerrycare fer the Old and I spose Pubicare fer the yung, but all they got now is ther Bloo Crotch. Meddlycare wuz never on Runny Ragin's gender before, but ther's a leckshun cumin up and hospiddle costs are sore-in. Why do you think all them docters wares masks like hiway rubbers? To pay fer ther golf carts not to menshun them Expensive Care Eunicks with ther Cathouse Scanners and the cardlio-vaseline sturgery with the angrio-plastickseen lithotrips fer transplantin ther orgins all over the place. Wat ever happen to goozgreese and fryer's ballsome?

I jist cum back frum lookin in on the wife on her bedda pane. She is lookin better than she were, tho to tell you the trooth she don't look as well as she wuz before she got as bad as she is now. I jist put a musterd plaster on her, but weer outa yer Keens so I slap on sum Hellmanmayonaze. Tomorra I'le probly have to go to yer Handyhoam hardwares fer to git sumthin to nock the dam plaster off cuz it givs her a lousy hedake, so mebby I shud mix up a cock-stale of homoselzer and flee powder.

The docter jist called, and tole me I shud giv Valeda a hot bath before retire-in. Well, ther's no hurry fer that. I don't plans to re-tire fer anuther cuppla yeers.

69

12.
Sittin on De Fence

Our nashnul helth is not wortha pincha coonsh if we terns around and makes ashes of arselfs in a nukuler wore. We bin staivin that off fer morn farty yeers, but the thing as skeers everybuddy nowadaze is Terrierism.

Wen I wuz a lad terrierism jist ment razin up a buncha puppies, and P.L.O. wuz sumthin our teecher put on the blackbored so us moniters wooden rub it off. But everybuddy noes it now as yer Palestine Libation Orgy, run by Yassir Arrofat, that lil fella with the scraggily stubbil hoo looks like a ringer fer that old Beatleboy Ringer Starr if he wuz warin a Peezy Hut tabelcloth on his hed. They got branches all over the place with better attendants figgers than our Canajun Leegions, frum Tunas neer More-ocko to yer Seeriac hed sitty, Damasskiss. But the cheef trubbelmakers seems to be them offshits of yer Ayetoleyuh Cockamamie hoo has spred out all acrost yer MidEest, and probly gun in fer to git into yer Midwest, like yer profit Mahomit Allee dun a thousand yeer ago. I don't meen that hevvywate hoose A.K.O. Cashyus Clay, but mind you, he's

Bringin in the sheekels.

1 of them Muslins neals down and faces the berthplace of Mecka oinkmint every day at 5 o'clock.

But sum of these fannyticks wuz wat Runny Ragin musta bin aimin at wen he bommed yer Libberers, in a attemp to make Kernal Kadaffy Fried Chicken. It wuz the same plains lader appeer in that moovy last yeer, "Top Gum". That prooves life is reely like yer moovys, witch is wat Runny alwaze bleeved. Ware do you think he got the idee fer his Star Wars in the firsplace? And wen he wuz watchin the "Rambone" with Slyvester Stallion playin a Murine went back to Veet Napam and won that war the Yanks lost ten yeer ago, Ronny tern to his Nanny and sed: "Now I noe how to git all them sostages frum out between yer Lesbiansnees!"

That bomming sure skeered everbuddy fer a wile, speshully yer alleys of Runny Ragin, eggsept Marg Snatcher hoo ain't skeered of nobuddy, and hoo wood bom the Focklins off any forner quick as lick at them. But the eeziest thing in the world fer yer terrierast gorillas is to pick off anuther sostage all by hisself standin on a Bayroot Street, so Runny deeside anuther tackytick. He use the seecrite weppin that has maid Amerca grate—cold cash. So the mewsick change frum "Rocky, Too" to "Heer Cums the Bribe", and alluva suddin it was Arms fer the luv of Allah. It maid Tricky Nixy's Watery Gait look like a tupperware party.

Is this Kernel a nut?

But the mane thing we lernt about Terrierism is that the dam thing is Big Bizness like Genial Motors or ye Mafiascos. Them Arrafatfiters is sittin on ther assets up to 5 billyun doller, rite up ther with yer Forchune-it 500 cumpnys. Accorn to "reely-eye-abull sorces", they gits most of ther investers not frum the Kadavry Kernel, or yer Serviet Onion, but frum the reel Sheek peeple in yer Keywait and yer Shoddy Arapeyuh. And ther now gittin into liggiterit bizness the same way as yer Cosy Nostrils.

And wat about round my incesters ole naberhood, Bellyfast. Not oney are yer I.R. Ates gittin into perteckshun rackits, gammlin, nite-clubs, but now they're settin up a tacksy-cab bizness by bommin all the busses. And hoo do ya think is in key-hoots with them but ther belubberd innimys yer PUDFers, Prodda-stance Ulcer Defents Farce. And them two arched ryevills bin workin a bilding frod that syfin off 60 millyun in tackses frum yer Infernal Revenyou and they split the profets. Wen you see bildins burnin in the Londonderry air, it's jist millinary rivals on both sides workin *together* on a prosess of limination on ther bizness compytishun.

Mind you, if yer talkin grave issyuhs, the reel hore story is still that war between them stale mates, yer Earaker and yer Eyeranner. It's bin goin on longern World War 2, and they're usin pizen gas frum World War 1. That cums pritty close to home fer me, cuz I wunts seen this Vet sellin pensills on Worrier's Day at yer Tronto Exjibishnists, and this fella wuz coffin his lungs out as he stud ther. I figgerd he musta had tubercolossus, but my Dad tole me had bin giv mustered gas at Eep, witch is spelt Ypres, but shood be call Wipers cuz that's wat it dun to our boys. It didden exackly kill this pore devil, but by swinjer it mite as well of fer the coffin he hadda put up with.

That kinda pizen wuz outlord by yer Ginheaver Convenshunals over to Swishyland long bout 19 & 25, but that didden stop it bein use by yer Japanee in Chiner, yer Eyetalian in Abaseenya, and roomers of it in Veet Napam, Camboatyuh and Louse. And Sadman Insane yer Earaker got so desprit aginst that old Hy Mullah Howmany that he sed he'd go into any exstream, and looks like he did. And in retalianation them Eye-ranners thru in ther secreet weppin, childern, every little wun beleevin they wud go to Muslin hevven firsclass jist like them Kammykrazy pile-its in ther Japannd Zeeros, or them oldtime Scandalnavyuns, the Vikings with the horny hats goin to ther Valhalla Inn-the-sky.

Mosts wars seems to be fot over how to warship our Maker. I never heerd of a buncha athywists or agnosticleticks git het up enuff fer to sholder arms and march agin eech uther. No wunder our speechies is call Homo Sappyuns. Yer Untide Nations aint bin abel to stop enny conflicks sints yer Norse-Souse Kareerwore in yer erly 50's.

It jist goze to proove wat we shooda noan. Wars is waged cuz its good fer wages. War is a expansiv groath industery and the last thing yer arm sailsmin wants is fer peece to brake out. Yer Krumlin and yer Pantlegon atween em sudsidizes most of yer army-mint makers, the one guvmint-run, the ladder yer privates enteraprize. But with them both, wore is a side-issyuh. The Roosians arm therselfs in case all ther peeple gits revoltin at the saim time, and yer Staits needs guns fer there state relijun, wich is Aunty-Commonism.

And now Ronny Ragin wants us to up our Armed Farces in exchange fer him not droppin Assid Rane. Ronny is cumfurtabull around them armymint millyumairs, almost as much as old Hollowood acters. He never reely got much acksun durin Wirld War One-One; insted he wuz makin little doctordementerys fer yer armfarces. The oney big millinery shampane he got in on wuz yer Operayshin Grenade, a little topical place beween Trinitydad and Barbydose, and not far frum them ilands wants to join up with us, yer Turkey Cacas.

Runny evaded yer Grenade'uns without so much as a fonecall to any of his alleys. Marg Snatcher got a mite hufty, cuz them Grenades use to be Birdish, part of our Cuminyerwelth, but they seprated and bin livin in Anarkicky ever sints, first to yer rite and then to yer lefty. Runny thot they was gittin too handy-in-gluv with them Cubists, and Ragin is a old Castrohater frum way back. So he sent in his A-Teem fer to swot the place jist like on the TV. Mebby he wuz gonna hav a iland evasion every weak, until it wood be a 26-weak serious like his old "Dedvally Daze" or the "Genial Eclectic Theater".

Canajuns is thot of in the wirld as a nice neutered peeple, but evryeer we sells a billyun $$ of arm-mints. Missyiles

Sanbaggin yer crooze missal.

75

keep croozin all over Elberta. That's cuz Ronny thinks the low-cal ideel cuz it reminds him of yer Serviet Roosia, speshully the parts in Sighbeerier jist beyond yer Urinals. Yer crooze don't work too good in forsted arias and unflat toppleograffy cuz yer missyile don't noe yer woods frum yer mountings. And they gotta flys low to the ground fer to avoid sneek preevews. She's a ittybitty of a thing compair to yer Intracounterrental B.M.'s, but tho' yer crooze is small it's still first strike and yer out.

And hoo giv Ronny permishun fer all this croozin? Don't blaim his No. 1 fan, Briney Bullroney. It wuz Peeair Idiot Terdo dun it all by hisself 1 day wen the rest of yer Common House wuz on a reesess. But Briney cood do sumthin about this even now, cuz he got a lot more pull with Ronny than Pee Air ever did, hoo rite after that went runnin round the wirld lookin fer a little peece, and got a prize fer it even if he didden find any. He even yell at Marg Snatcher wen she cum to Canda, shoutin that he wanted her "bustin her ass fer peece". She never giv him nyther.

But all that's gon by yer broads, and I jist wish Briney wood tock to his old pal and dementor Ronny about the croozin, and tell him that Canda ain't atall like Roosia, not by a bullshot. Fer 1 thing we don't have no secrete pleece like them Cagey Beegees. We tride it with yer C-SISsys, but they never got no unyforms and mosta them is tryna defecate back to yer R.C.'s M.P.'s And more importint, them Reds is all aythywists, they don't bleeve in a Soopream Bein. (We got rid of ours on Leepyeer Day '84 and now he's a consitooshunal liar in Muntryall.)

Altho' he tride to cut down our Armed Farces and git us off our Natoes, it wuz Peeair spent five billyun doller fer 1 plain, yer CF-18, witch has certny terned out all its crack up to be, speshully yer tale seckshun. It's a jetsetter, and so is Pee Air, witch is mebby why he spent all our munny on it. Not without testin it first tho', fer pert neer 12 minit. That's

76

Prime Mistress Snatcher hoists herself on the poles.

5 billyun spent on them jetsetters that dint leeve nuthin fer
to spend on our Seenyer Serviss.

So far the West Edmingtun Shoppin Mall has got more
slubmarines than the hole of yer Canajun Navels. So if
them Rooskys ever evade us, let's hope to Gawd they wanna
go shoppin. Wen Ministerd of Defents Pairn Beady wuz ast
in Kwesting Peeriod wat plans he had fer to re-eekwip our

navy, he anserd: "Friggit!" We only got 1 Corvet left, and I betcha we cant afford to git anuther 1 even holesail frum Genial Motors. If we sell off our old destroyers I hope we don't sell it fer junk like our aircrap carrier yer Bunnyventure. I think we cud git more fer our Navy if wee sole them all off as jennywine anteeks. We cood toss in fossils frum yer Senit and mosta yer Cabnuts too.

Our new offensive Minster Pairin Beety brung out his Wite Paper fer to start with cleen sheets, the first in 16 yeers. He wants to spend the next 5 billyun dollers of our tax munny on ten nukuler slubmarines fer to take keer of our Sovrintitty under the hardnin of yer Articks ice. But them suckers of subs is fit fer fightin' not perteckshin. I'd jist as soon them haffprice deezels instedda spendin all that cash on hand-to-mouth cat-in-mouse Brinksmanship. But the reel reezin fer puttin Canajun nukuler subs up in yer hy Articks is not fer spyin on the Rossians but fer to keep the Yanks frum stick in ther polar prows up our cold passages. Isn't that kinda eckspentsif snoopyervisishun wen we cood jist tern on the radiar?

We got 76,908 arm and 7,724 arm wimmen, and Pairn wants more wimmin, more Prserves, and more convention weppins. But he don't want no more Norway, so he's takin' 5,000 of our fellas (and girls?) outen the place and shippin then over to Germny, cuz it took too long fer to ship our droops over frum Canda, cuz they arrive 2 weaks late at a wore exercise last yeer. But Germny is even further frum Hallyfacks. Don't ask me. Wores don't make sents to a fella hoose tryna bring sumthin' outa the ground insted of leevin a lotta holes. But I peefurs them convention weppins to yer horeheds, cuz in a nukuler wore its first strike and yer both out, and that'll be bedtime fer all us Bonzos.

Funny thing, I herd a roomer frum one of our D.V. Ayshunists in the Departmint of Vetrans Havin Affairs, that Ottawar has spent 50 millyun doller undoing yer Uenuchficatin Pogrom. Ya mind in '67 wen we dress all our soljers sailers and airyplane fellas in the same green garbidge bags, and maid them look lik they shood be taggin cars in fronta parkin meeters? Now they're gonna go back to ther kiltses and bellybottom drores. It'll probly help keep the peece, cuz cum Sardy nites they'll be too bizzy brollin with eech uther in a pub fer to git into trubble anywares elts.

Now that NASA's in the cole cole ground, mebby its gud that wer gittin back to convenshunal armymints instedda all this spaced out hi-tex stuff. I still wisht Runny and his Nanny hadn't bin watchin wen Luke Slywalker and Oaky Bin Naskokey took ther lit up sords and beet the helmit offa that Garth Invaider. Becuz that's how Runny hopes to deel with yer Reds, feechering spaced-out cumbats with them lazy beams that acts like a flashlite in heet.

And he wants us to go along with him, cuz he feels we ain't pullin our wates wen we stands on gards fer thee and him. It's troo only yer Leechesteens and Luxybergers spends less on ther defensivness per squair hed than us duz. Even yer Swede and yer Swish has morn us, and we got nuthin like a Dane with ten time more armied preserves than we has. Its troo, we is all lyin down on the job countin on yer Yank fer to sit up and do it all fer us. Wat Canda needs is its own sit-down army that'll stand up fer us wen our time cums. Bleeve me, ther's nuthing like a taist of armied life to make a yung fella depreeshiate his own home.

Now I'm no patsyfist, and even if I wanted to be, wores is never gonna stop. They bin goin on ever sints Cane hit Mabel. Jist human nurcher I spose, but if they ever plans anuther drop like yer Herosheeny or yer Naggersocky, it's lites out everybuddy. But that don't meen we shooden gard our harths, homes, and hertage in case we don't git any nukeys.

"Let them fergit, let them fergit" seems to be the reel massidge on November 11 these days. Hardly nobuddy stands stil fer 2 minits anymore. Wirl Wore 1 is so fur back, most yung peeples got ther minds on the big 1 comin up. And hoo kin blaim em? After goin to the moovys they probly feels they livs on a dethstar. And now we got a millyun and a haff times yer kickpower of them Heerosheeny bums. Enuff to kill us all twenny time over frum eether sides.

Now it's no more mewchewal detergents, like Henry Kissassinger set up. Runny Ragin wanted to get supeerier, and he felt we wuz all behind yer Serviets. I wunder how Runny felt wen that teenyager frum West Jermny pennytrated yer Roosian defentses and floo his liddle Sessner rite into Red Squair and parked it oppsit yer Krumlin. Them Rooskys was seein red wen they sent off a cuppla ther feeld-marshalls off to Sibeerier for a yeer round winter hollyday and sum refeshin corses in yer nashnul securatitty.

Call me a peesmunger, but I'm no dum tool of yer Serviets hoo wants to drop our gards so they kin infilthitrait us with ther fifth colyumist. But I'm not lookin forerd to wat Ronny and Casper Whineybugger is plannin up in yer statusfear.

Lazybeam War between asternuts circumsizing the erth in tin cans is gonna refleck down on us all, and don't expeck no help fer yer woonded cuz they got no space fer stretchers in space. The Pantlegon clames they will use them roboats fer to remove yer disable back to sum spaced stayshin. I got a better idee. Why not let them roboats do all the fytin, and I don't care how fur out they gits. They kin do it behind Marse or even up around Yuranus, jist as long as the rest of us kin sit home and watch it on the TV like sum Intur-Galexlaxic Soopybowl. Hoo needs anuther war down heer wen we still got intynashnul terrierism and wirld cup socker? Let's hope we all freeze our nukes off before that big atomical winter sets in and we live in Oblivia ferevernever.

13.
Bumper to Bumper Crop

Canda's northland seems to be anywares a hundert mile north of yer 49 parrylells of lassitewd. In the fewcher weer gonna be the bufferin stait tween yer Yank and yer Serviet, and they're alreddy refurbishin the ole Dewdew line. Canda is becummin a kind of frozen bananner republick, and the forn cars heddin our way is the oney bumper to bumper crop that's worth cultyvatin any more. Round our parts, all us fokies frum Muskokies never disgusts farmin no more; the tock is all tooryism.

And its not yer urbane parts tooryists is flockin to see, it's us roorals, cuz our sitties cant hold a rockit to ther metropopolitan senters down ther fer illissitt nite-life. To Yanks we are still that undy-sivillized big game preeserve nex door, a place to get away frum it all fer at leest 2 weaks. They wanna use our parts as a tempry rest-home. The time seems to be rite fer that, with morn more of our nabers crowdin into yer downtowns of this country, makes the cuntryside a lot more tranquwillize.

I wisht in a way I had never staid on the farm, but insted

got me a gas stayshin franchfrise frum yer Golf or yer Taxco or even yer Peterocan. I cood sit by the pumps and watch all them toorsts drive up fer to fill ther tanks and drane ther famly. The wife and f.s. throws 1 of the best spreds on the rode durin our anal harvist gangthrash, so Ide set her up in a stand with her hotmeet pize, so that her cussedomers cood eet and git gas at the same time. Reezin them Yanks uses up so mutch gass is them rode sines they sees on our hywaze. Merkens is used to seein 55 mph, so wen they see 100 kmh they think it meens a hunnert Kanajun miles an hour, which is why they tares up our rodes like it wuz the Injunapples Speedway.

Visiters thinks our parts is offally seenick. We even has familyer strangers frum the sitty keeps cummin back yeer after yeer; so I keeps a rodeside stand fer fresh vegibles. The 1 thing all them toorsts asks is if I'm orgazmic wen I farms. I thot they ment the stuff we giv the bull on the fly frum Spane, but all they reely wants to fine out is if our vegibles was razed in pestysides or jenuwine animal matters. I tell them its jist plain horeshit, and they buy the stuff happy as hawgs in heet. Then Sundy nite they go back to ther smoggy sitty that has a brown cloud hangin over it wood choke a bull.

The wife and f.s. wishes I had never tuck up the farm ware my fourbears left off. She'd druther hav run a conveenient store, and that way we mite a kep the sun and hare of our holy marcaroni, Orville, intrusted in stayin with the Farquharson famly bizness. But Orville thinks he's gonna becum a big rottenroller like that Bruise Stingspleen and he won't stop pickin at his twanger. But he'll probly end up in a foredoller a hour job with Wensdy's or Mickdonald or yer Burglerkings.

Oh my gol, my Fur Sail sine has bin up lesson a weak, and I jist got a offer fer parta my estaits! The Parry Sound golf corse butts rite on to my hardwood bush. It's oney bin

82

*John and Chills Turner at ther lokul soop kitchin (just a
Stornaway).*

goin a few yeers, but is poplar, and now they wants to
enlarge ther holes. I bin gettin 1 or 2 of them ballersa day
over the fents into my bush, straying offa the strait and
narra and endin up on ther hands and nees lookin fer a wite
dot in a cowpad.

Even before yer verminal equalnuts, or yer first robbin
and yer first lode of fertlyizer, golfballers is yer first sine of
spring. They cum draggin ther club bags behine them, ter-

nin over the ground with ther mashers and nibblenicks. I allus follows them later with a lardcan witch fills up with doowurms. Mind you, it takes golfers all summer to tern over as much as I kin do with a cultyvater in 1 afternoon. But they tell me the idee of the game is not splittin up diggots, but gettin in the hole. My gol, I jist dun that with a hundert aker farm.

Now I don't noe nuthin about this golfball game, I wooden noe witch end of yer caddy yuh grabs aholt of. But I don't see the sens of takin 18 akers of good pastyerland and fillin it fulla holes jist so sum mid-aged biznessmen kin hav a few strokes. And like liddle kids they seems to spend most of ther time in the sand. But they don't calls it sand, they calls it a bunker. Ain't that ware Hitler commit sewerside?

Th'idee of the game is to git yer ball frum yer tee to yer cup, morn a hunderd rod away. Valeda thinks the tee wood git cold before it gits in yer cup, but I tell her it's not that kinda tee. It's a liddle thumtack you places under yer balls before you drives off. (She so golf-iggerunt she thinks a Challenge Cup is a pair of brassears).

Wen I wuz a yung fella, athaletics wuz the nicest way of gittin exosted if you wuzn't alreddy married. But Valeda thinks that golf is jist a excuse fer a lotta men to walk around in funny close with a strange bag. It looks like a lotta work to me, like bein a postman, a carpit beeter and a ditch-digger all at once, sept you carrys even more tools and you hav to ware them horny shoes on yer bottoms.

But mosta them golfers don't hardly walk anymores. They sit on these little go-go carts looks like the toy cars they got on yer Exhibishunists Middleway, ware you pays 75 sents fer to cram yerself into these tiny rigs and then you go careemin around tryin to whang yers into the tuther fellas as hard as billy-o. That don't make no more sens to me than yer golfball game, cuz I see peeple doin the same thing fer free on yer Horeway 69.

84

Them golfers is sposed to play yer fareway but it don't sound like that to me. Ther's more bull on ther side of the fents then mine wen they counts up ther scores. They shouts "fore!" swings six and then puts down 2. This is calld improoving yer lie. Then they has the gall to tell you the Bibel tells them so, and they qwotes Sam 23: "He maketh me to lie, down in green pastyers wen my cups runneth over."

Sundyscool tot me to be a strait shooter and not a hooker, but the only 2 good balls I ever hit wuz the day I step on our garden rake by misteak. Golfers is never in cherch on Sundy but they clames they is relijuss anywaze, with ther heds bowed, ther hands clasp as if in prair. If you ast me ther jist playin a round.

Scotsmin clame to hav invent 3 things: curlin, golf and wisky. I'm not too sure about anythin but the wisky. Yer first golfgame wuz sposed to of bin plaid after a dinner giv in onner of ther grate Scotch poewet, Rabbi Burns. In his mammary they brung out a hagass, witch terns out is a kinda porritch maid frum the guts of a sheep and soke inyer hy spearits. But non of them gests had the guts to eet it, and they felt so blaim sheepish they all hit it with ther wonky wockin sticks till it got small enuff fer to fall in a hole in the flore. That wuz sposed to be yer first holin one. But the game cot on cuz Scotsmen wuz tired of gitten hernyas frum tossin off ther tellyfone poles.

That's as maybee, but I seen a moovy on the TV wuz one of them sighence frickshun rangdangdoos call "2 thou pluss 1" that wuz mostly about yer fewcher but start out in yer pastyer. At the start of the pitcher a buncha pre-histercle chimp-pansys wuz jumpin around in the hy grass with nuthin much to do, the stait of employmint lookin to be bout the same back then as it is in yer Martimes now. Alluva sudden 1 of them grillas picks up a bone of a old Brontysore and start to wirl it round his hed. Fer sum reesin classified mewsick plaid by a simpathy orkester starts and a big black bildin lookin like Tronto's Teediuss Bank shoots outa the erth behind this munky, but he pays it no mind, even tho' that mewsick musta grab him by the dessaballs. But by circumsizin this bone over his hed he axidently decapassitated 1 of his fella chimp with it, and it roll down a hole into yer valleyblow. That's why these beests wuz call yer missing links. Accorn to sum Darwun's theery the reezin they stood up on ther hine laigs and staid that way wuz they got intrusted in yer baysick drives. And so they musta fullfill man's erlyist dreem, to say ereckt at all times. Them as staid down with ther nuckles on the ground probly becum football plairs.

14.
Athalettickle Support

Ther's mebby 2 uther ways of gittin to be filthyrich left in this country of ars. Nummer 1, if yer nummer ever cums up, is yer Lottrees. The twennieth senchury wuz sposed to belong to us, but I think it cood end up belongin to Blotto Canda. Mebby that's why everybuddy seems to be a fool fer a pool these daze and I don't meen the kind ya pore yer chorines in. They'll plunk down ther shackles regler fer a longshot even tho' they got more chants of becummin Prime Minster, witch is 1 in 25 millyun—but nobuddy wants that job after wat happen in the poles to poor Briney Bullroney.

So every weak its a Lottermainyuh, dip into yer pigbank then scratch'n show. I use to have a fludder on them old Irish Sweepsteaks but it oney cost 2 doller a yeer. And you hadda be offal carefull if ya won cuz the hole deel was illeagle and you cooden let yer slips show. But now every provinss is bildin up sum kinda Hairystage Fund to pay fer ther defickates.

Mind you, winnin has its own problems. No sooner do you cum to clect, than they flashes you with that first polarhemroid and you becums a targit about to be inunderdated by vackyume sailsmen. And better take armgards with youse, cuz yule be follerd by every relltiv hangers-on yuh ever met in yer life. The 1 bunch that cant put the arm on yuh is yer Revenhoors fer yer prize is taxabull-free. But they'll git you laider, by hooker by crooks.

The only uther way of gittin over and into yer lifestiles of yer ritchly infamous is thru athleets feats. My boy Orville seems to be a hi-scorer, on his weakends. He won't take a backseet to no one, but he don't play outdoor sports. If I wuz his age I'd spend all my spairtime slapshootin a horesbun agin a barndore. Not in the summertimes mebby, works better in yer friggid wethers. But I think the oney chants fer a farmlad today is gittin into 1 of them minermidgyhocky teems and be seen by sum good ole scout hool send him up to yer mayjer leegers or even yer NH Hellers, and the lad becums a millyunair or at leest a thousandair.

In Maxyco them poor pee-ons trys to git ritch by bein a bullfitter. Its a bit like goin in fer pollyticks, sept that in Maxyco after you throws yer hat in the ring you has the bull thrown at you insted of the vicey of yer versy. I spose pollyticks has allus bin the oldest way of gittin in the gelt, tho prosseltooshun is sposed to of bin at it before our delected repryehnsitivs. But them two perfeshuns is linxed so close ennywaze, both of them by now is pritty well rooned by amachoors.

But hocky is how I wooda made my pile, insted of still shuvvlin it twicet a day. Its funny, most peeples thinks of hocky as Canda's nashnul sport. It aint. Its LaCrotch, wich is now mostly plaid indores. It was thunk up by our abridgeinall peeples lookin fer sumthin to do with ther snowshoos wen they got all warp. But them scalpers with the curv blaids never start up hocky. Tomahawky mebby. It

Lookin fer net profets.

wuz my incestral Ire-ishers start up all that hurling them-
selfs with sticks upon yer ice. The game wuz call shinty and
is still plaid today in parts of Norse Amurca like Noo Jerzy
and Pissberg, wher them poor Devvils and wingless
Pingwins had ther regler shinty seizin.

So by now you reelize it don't reely matter that we sold the Yanks hocky, and that ther hindquarters is now low-cate on yer Man Hatin Iland. That's wher them Saskytune orgynizers hadda go a few yeers back wen they wuz hopin to take over the Sin Loose Losers frum yer Poorina peeple. And at the start it look like they had everything by the bags. But wen they got down to Hindquarters they found that nun of them Nooyorkers had ever herd of a place call Saskytune, even tho all them Saskytooners had herd of Nooyork. So they ast the Kernel Kadavry of Canajun sport, Harld Ballhard fer to cum down and fill them in. Harld sure filld in Saskytune all rite, and it aint uncoverd sints, fer the big Ball Hard tole the NH Hell present encumberants, Johnny Zeegler, that the oney way yuh kin gits to that Saskytune in winter is by dogteem. And I spose Harld shud be the 1 to noe, he's led a teem of dogs fer yeers. Now John Bropey cum along fur to be coach. The wife took one look at him in his reverse greesyan formula and sed "No wunder them leefs is winnin! Lookit hoos in charge: Fill Dunny Hoo!"

Harld, yuh know, never wuz a hockyplair, he start out as a speed skater till they finely got him offa the drugs. Drugs seams to of becaim the slution fer all these sporty soopy-stars hoo gits overpaid and dunno wat to do with ther munny. But it's even happnin to sum of our Olimpricks can-dydaits hoo keeps dippin into them diabloical steeryos fer ther extry hoarmoans. I figger by the time they're reddy fer '88 it'll take a vetnairy-aryan fer to tell sum of our boys frum our girls. And they're not makin munny frum this goin thru the changes, cuz yer Olimprix is strickly hammer-chewer. I sure don't think a gold meddle is worth changin yer sex fer. Besides, sex changes is jist like any other athaletic competishun, its offen nip and tuck all the way.

Lets be honist, hocky is the oney expordabull sport fer us Canajuns. All the uther perfessional stuff we plays up heer is fulla Yanks sprinkle with a few toke-in Canajuns. Mind you, ther's allwaze the intersepshun that prooves yer brakin the rools, like that Norse Battlefort boy, Roob Maze, hoo last yeer wuz voted by the Yank feat-baller riters fer to be ther Nooky of the Yeer.

Our own featsballs is in a bad way now, with tock of committin merger with sum Yankyleeg like yer NFL or yer USFL sumtime before yer CF of L goze NSF. This is reely wat they calls, in hiclass litterchur, yer "Soopream Arny", on accounta Amerken futball got its start rite heer in Canda, not inyer Staits. Back in 18 ot 54, at MuntryAll's MickGill Universally, in the daze wen they still had all ther fackultys, they had a frenly game of socker with Harvord Colleejit. All of a suddin, fur no parent reesin, 2 of the Canajun plairs maid a pass at eech uther. This layin on of hands change ther hole lives.

And the game too. The Amerkins tuck up makin passes, but hadda change our tuff rools. We oney had 2 bucks and a kick fer to make 10 yard, they hadda inflait it to 4 bucks incloodin yer kicks. The Yank game went mosely on the ground cuz ther all bilt like tanks, wile Canajuns is more airy minded. The 1 unrit rool that stays the saim in the granstands of both cuntrys is that it is still sposed to take fore qwarters fer to finish off a fifth.

I like our Canajun game better on accounta I allways luvs to see sumthin go by air thats not gonna cost me 36 sents. Our game is menshun, by the way, in yer Noo Testymint: "And it caim to pass." That's next to yer Qwarterbacks Creed: "It is more blested to handoff than to reseeve."

Yer Gay Cup last yeer wuz won by that old baller Harld Ball Hard. Well, to be more exack it wuz his Humilton Pussycats that dun it, beetin the pads offa them Edmington Examoes. This yeer Harld has big plans fer to win agin. Any teem Harld runs has awreddy gon thru more coaches than a CNR conduckter, but wen Harld herd His Holeness yer

91

Ballhard sez it's a snap.

Pope wuz gonna revist Canda, he got the brite idee that if he cud derange a Massrally at yer Inever Winn Stayjun in Hamilton, Jon Pall 2 cud bless the teem and at the saim time teech them how to take a lot more convurts thru yer hevvenly goley post. Speekin of Canajun invenshuns like fit-ball, did yoo noze that krokeynole wuz invent over to Watterloo bout Conflagration Yeer by sum Mennanites? But the wun game that has never bin tuck up perfessyunal in this landa ours is baskybawl.

This bran noo game had its whirl premeer in Springfeeled Mass in 1891, but the fella hoo dreem it up was frum Almont, Ontaryo. Gym Naysmith wuz foolin round in a cherch basemint with a bullsbladder and a cuppla bushill baskit. He bloo up the bladder and put both them baskits at oppsit ends of that basemint. It wirked. He slamdunkt the wirld with sumthin noo, and them Massachewsuns new he wuz onto a good thing, but bein Yankys, they hadda thunk up sum improovmints. They thot the game wuz too Canajun, meenin too slow. Naysmith had orgynize 2 six-man

Rong baskit, wrong ball.

teems but them Yanks maid it a 5 man game, speedin the hole thing up by remoovin the goley outa the baskit. By that time he had alreddy put his feet thru the blame baskits ennywaze so the plairs didden hav to shinny up the pole eech time fer to git ther bladder back.

Canajuns tuck to the game rite away, speshully down in yer Marmtides ware its the Nummer one collitch sport. No perfessyunal teem has yet appeer sept fer a few exhibishunists games, but mebby that's cuz yer En Bee Ay aint too keen about expandin crost yer 49 parlells.

The sport at witch Canajuns generally end up nummer 1 in the wirld is yer Curlin. Canajuns has become the teem to beet in yer Sliver Brooms and yer Bryers. The wife and I likes to curl up together all winter with our own bumspeels, taking turns neelin down to git our rocks off wile the uther pardner brakes wind in front.

Now yer Scot has allus clame the fame fer thinkin up the game. Wen he cooden eet the wee wifey's scons he tuck em outside and slid em along the froze-over Furtha Forth with her chasin after him with a broom. But that's not wen the game start up. If yule look agin in yer Noo Testymint you'll find that Our Lord defers to curlin wen he wuz defendin that Woman of Sum Area at the well. He sed, and ya cood look Him up: "Let him hoo is without Sin, Cast the First Stone."

Smatter of fack, Curling started even afore yer *Old* Testymint, rite here in Canda. You mind the last Ice Age? (And I don't meen the winter of '87 in Sinjons, Nofunland.) I'm tockin bout a cuppla millenema ago wen sumbuddy tern down the wirld's thermalstat and everybuddy that had bin in heet cum all of a suddin over friggid. Canda wuz at that time enjoin a topical climacks, and our first sittizens wuz them prehysterical Land Rovers like yer bucktooth Tyger and yer hairy Mastoidon. Valeda sez she wood have hated livin back in them daze, at the murcee of yer ellafints. But wen the Big Freeze cum down on everythin but wageys and priceys, then this hole place shut down fer the seizin as soon as them glassyears cum down frum the Bafflin Bay and moove south fer the winter as fur as yer 49 parrlells of lassitewd. That made immygration our cheef export, and by the time that ice spred itself all acrost us frum Mare to Mare, we wuz not only friggid but uninhibited too.

Bimeby we got sum noo inhibitants, but not frum Yerp, frum Azure. They cum over as soon as they got ther Bering Strait, met up with sum uther forners, mebby on a daypass frum ther ships in Vancoover. They all got matey round the fire and, bang, ther wuz yer first natif-born Injun.

Ther wernt nothin fer to do, on accounta Canda wuz jist wun big rinka ice, and nobuddy yet had thunk up a Samboney. No uther jobs neether, the rate of B.C. unemployablemint bein about the same then as is now. All ther wuz lyin about on all that ice wuz a buncha rox had bin smooth round the edgies by ther erozenuss zones. With nuthin elts to do, them Injuns started heddin eest and playin with therselfs. That's why they becum to becalled yer Stoney Injun cuz they started to curl the toes offa yer Backfeet, by heevin ther stones on that ice.

It wernt till senturions later that yer Erl of Sellchurch brung the first Scotsettlers to Canda. By that time Curling wuz sentered on yer prayery, hard by Winnypeg, a nacheral ice-surfiss pert neer ten munth of the yeer, ware life is conveenyintly flat. And wen them first Scotsmin seen our Injuns neelin down fer to start ther bumspeels, they figgerd they wuz in on sum relijus rang-dang-doo. But wen they seen our oridgeinal peeples havin fun at it, them Scotch wanted to horny in on it too. But them Clamsmen wuzn't drest fer the perseedins; they wuz warin them liddle miniskirts and nuthing undyneeth but ther shoosin stockins. The first time them pore bandylaiged buggers bent over in a noreast gail it wuz game over.

Canajuns has reely tuck to Basebawl even tho they had nuthin to do with its creemation. But then hoo reely did? It wuz spose to hav bin invent by a Amerken, Abner Dubblehedder, but if yiz take a look at yer famly Bibel, yule find yer Yank is tockin thru his cap. Yuh don't hav to look far fer to find how baseball start up. It's on the first page, first chapper, even yer furst vurse of the Book of Gennysez. Ile jist pick out the hedlines fer yuh: *In the big inning. Eve stole first, Adam stole second. Cane give Abel a bass hit. Dave-id struck out Go-lieth. The Prodiggle Sun run fer home. Rachel went to the well with the pitcher.*

Wat Canajuns is waitin fer is the day yer first Wirld's Seerious ends up here tween yer Blooeyjays and yer Exposers. Fer wun thing, it cud solv all the langridge problims in Cuebeck.

Haff the Wirld Serious games wud be in Tronto, and haff in Muntryall, and ile bet all Canda wud try to git to see them. Now if you wuz sittin in that Olimpricks Stayjun on a cool Ocktober day, and yuh felt like sumthin fer to warm up yer gut, yuh wooden say, "Boy, gimme a hot dog!" Nosirree, fer that's agin the law. Insted yuh wave at the dogseller and say "Gerkin icky. Oon Cheyenne choode, essveepee." If we all spoke the Garlick langridge the same way Long John Doofenbeeker use to say it, or mebby Bricey Mickissassey still duz, by the end of that afternoon the intire provinshuls of yer providince of Cuebec wood be speeking Anglish outa pure self-defents.

This yeer they put the cap on ther Olimprick playpen. That big rig of Jeens Dropouts never did git finish wen it wuz maid in '76. Not jist the cuvver up-top. The reezin most fans sat on ther edge of ther seets fer ten yeers wuz not cuz the games wuz so intrustin and eggsite-in, but becuz them contrackters had never put in no warshrooms. It wernt like Ontaryario; ther wuz a place to stand, but no place to go.

Domes is all the outrage with yer in-crowds of athaletic supporters. First wun in Canada wuz that big Woopy cushin out to Vancoover. Did you see that sucker blow up on yer Teevy? Shure showed the power of inflayshin in this cuntry. Then nex cum the 1 Caligary got fer playin hocky in. It's call yer Saddledome. Probly got named the day after the laidest Don Geddy bludget cum out, and them taxpayers finely got the bill. Seems to me the wun place in Canda cud do with a big cuvver-up is Edmington, the home ware yer Exximoes roam, but I spose it'll go on bein yer hemroid capital of the wirld.

Tronto is the place has the flimsyist eggscuse fer havin a Dome. Oh, I noe ther wuz a freezability studdy maid prooving that the reezin all Tronto fans is Bloo is cuz they keep gittin chilld in ther bleechers. On openin day wen them 48 Hi-Landers is marchin about in ther kilts and squeezin ther bags to play yer "Bloo Bells of Scotland" they looks like they reely meen it.

But the reel reezin fer this 250 millyun-or-so dollerprojeck wuz the day all that Yanky hankypanky happen in the park. Big Daisy Winfeel wuz outstandin in his feeld and absent-mind-like thru his bawl up in the air. It hit a seagle square amidshits and the pore berd hit the ground non-compost-deementis. Do you noe wat the gud peeples of Tronto wanted to do then? Put Winfeel in jail fer sixty days and take that alreddy ded bird to a hospitable! So Trontuh deeside it want a big cuvver-up. Then coum the problum of ware to put the blaim thing. They had 3 er 4 commitys drew up fer to serch fer a low-cal. Ther wuz plenny of suggestivs, but the final incishun plased it in downtown TO, rite nex to the Excommunicashun Tower, the biggest ereckshun Tron-toney-uns ever got. Mebbe the idee wuz to mate the 2 of them and spon a buncha lidldomes at the same time, witch cood be french-eyzed all acrost Ontarryo.

Fur a long time you wooden have noan the thing frum a

Bloojay prooves that lacrotch is still our nashnul sport.

hole in the ground, but then it started to take shape frum the ground up. That stayjum ground, by the way, is not gonna be orgasmickly natural fer to slide into, but is gonna be that haff-Aster turf that givs all the plairs carpit burns like they wuz playin florehocky without pads. I persnally wooden play on sumthin that my cattel wooden eet, but I gess econocomicks rools over athleats feats.

Nex cum a contest fer to giv the big dome a name. Sum sed it shood be name after the preevous encumbrance of the province, the Budda of Brampton, Billy Davis; uthers sed it shood be after the Left-handed guvner that wuz, John Black Aird. Sum sed it shood be after the Soopermayer of

Metropoppolitan Tronto, Paul Godfrey, now publisher of the little Sun paper that everytime you opens it ya git a bust in the face and uthers fayverd the curnt mare of Tronto, Arty Egglesome. But it ain't gonna be yer Billydome, or yer Airdome, or by the grace of Godfrey, yer Sundome, or even yer Godfreedome, or yer Eggdome. But the name pick out of a hat wuz yer Skydoam, witch had alreddy been run up the Flag Staff in Arsezona. So they shood add a extry vowel movemint and call it yer Sky-hi Doom, on accounta the bludgit fer this blaim thing keeps goin thru the roof.

Harld Ballerd wanted to name it after his deer frend, King Clantsy, but ther's awreddy a Kingdome cum to them Seattlers. Most peeple is awreddy callin it after the little Majer hoo foundered yer Make Beleaf Gardings in the firsplace, Conny Smythe. More and more peeple are standin lookin at that big hole and sayin': "That'd be yer big Con Dome."

15.
Histry of Yer Free Traid

Ther wuz a roomer that Tronto's Dome Stayjim wuz never gonna git to be bilt ther atall. That's on accounta they got a roof on it ware ther gonna be abel to push the skin back on a sunny day. That's why the hole rang-dang-doo wuz roomered to be flone to Ottawar and place rite over the Common House. Partly so Briney Bullroney cood feel safe under the Dome, cuz everything wood be retractabull, and partly cuz Milly wanted privatesee fur to carry on with the infeerior desecration she had had dun up yer 24 SuckSex Drive.

That's wher they had all them extry big cubberds bilt fer to take care of all Briney's loafers. Now I'm not tockin about the Aids that he got in his office. I'm tockin about all them shoos he owns, jist like that Fullapeenis woman hoo got imelded to Highwayuh with her little dickey-tater hus-bin, Fernand the Bully.

Briney's also bin havin trubble handling his huge cockus, witch is yer party git-toogether wher they uses a wip to make shur everybuddy cums. Mind you, the leeder of the Oppsit Posishun, yer Jonturner, is havin even wurse

Milly discusses her SusSex drives with her inferior desecrator.

trubble, cuz his is split down the middel. So between the 2 cockasses ther's a lotta trubble stirrin. Yer DP leeder, Eds Brod'sBent, seems to be in complete yewnicky with his party, cuz ther approach is wat you calls idiot-logickle.

And wat's the burr under all these asses? Free Traits with yer Staits. The idee is that if we kin eeliminate all our tarf barryers with yer Yanks, and it works, then we're gonna try the saim blaim thing tween the provinsses of this cuntry. So far, oney Noo Humpsure is kinda intrusted.

We bin tockin bout this kind of derangement even before Sir Jonny Mickdonald led us thru his Golden Archys of Conflagellation and spred our sezme seed bums frum see to see. It start up first jist after Grate Britten repeeled all her Cornlaws back in 1846. Wat them repeelers giv up wuz ther prefrince fer Canda, so nacherly all we cud do wuz start makin goo-goo eyes at yer Ewe Ass. Didden take long afore they wuz makin goo-goos back at us, mostly cuz we wuznt yet a cuntry and Amerkens had a Manyfist Dustiny fer to aynex us as ther next stait. In 1854 we ackshully sined a Restaprostity Treety but the hole thing got canseld by the Yanks jist after ther Sibble War.

That's wen old Sir John Eh yanked back frum yer Yank and replace all that Rustyprostity with his "Nasty-nil Polissy", and put up yer Grate Wall of Tarfs, so's we cud perduce frum our own factrys. Minit he sed that, about a millyun Westerners jumped acrost the boarder into the Staits.

In them days yer Grits wanted Free Traid and yer Torys wuz agin it. Sir Wifull Lorry Eh, tuck over after Sir John Eh and laid his derryair on the line fer Free Traits. The Yanks at that time coodna cared less; they wuz too bizzy tryna aynex Maxyco. Mind you, the deel Sirwilf work out cum 1911 wuz the best we ever cooda git: Rejuiced tarfs on Yank goods but most Canajun wuns wuz aloud to remane. Wen we axersize our frenchfries that yeer, the Grit slowgo wuz "Canda fer all Canajuns". The hed Tory, Sir Rubbert Bordeom, anser back that it wuz mornlikely "Canda fer 2500 Canajuns", meenin the big bizness tyfoons. The offishul Tory slowgo wuz "No Truckin Traid with Yanky Hanky Panky".

Wat's the reel issyuh? Canda has allwaze wanted more traid with yer Staits, wile all the Staits wants is jist Canda (or at leest our nacheral resorses: wadder, wood, minerables, and that lil TV fellar Mikejay Focks). They liked us better wen we wuz jist a colny, the oney wun that never got revoltin. Eeven our own histerians sed that as far as them Yanks is consern we wuz jist hoors of wood with our drores fulla watter. Mebby a lot of us is reddy to becum colnists agin, even tho it tuck us morn a hunderd yeer fer to git our own Constitooshunal, witch the Yanks had had sints they got borne. But morn a few Canajuns thinks that Pee Air Idiot Terdo brung that old peesa paper back frum Angland

102

Ed Broadsbent gits a gut feelin frum a pole.

jist to make a lotta work fer him and his fella corprit liars,
cuz if you gotta beef agin the guvmint based on them noo
Rites, yuh gotta go to cort, mebby all the way up to them
Soopreems in the red dresses, and that takes hunnerds of
thousands of dollers in liars fees. Cuz if you gits in fronta a
jedge, you need a dubbletalk experk fer to help you waid
thru all them "ware-asses and howsumevers and not-with-
standing moreovers theretoo." The Yanks got ther Consitooshunal by havin a revolushun, not sittin in the Common
House fer a hunderd yeer hopin to pass a movemint on the
floor.

Back in yer urly thurtys we had lotsa traid with our
nabers but it wuz mostly illissid. Farmers got even lesson
they gits now fer ther grane, but big bootlagers wud turn it
into Pro-inhibishun hooch, and roar backinforth crost our
boarders with it. Cum the fortys we wuz too bizzy on both
sides becummin yer Arsanall of Demockersy and yer bred-

baskit of the wirld. We wuz deep in dett all thru them Wore yeers but mostly to ourselfs thru Vickery bonds so it didden matter. And we had rashinin of butter and meets, so everybuddy went out and plant a Vickery gardin, and the hole cuntry becaim self-defishunt, mostly cuz ther wuz nuthin elts to do.

Longbout 1947, Mickenzy King, hoo sum Grits calls the Abie Linken of Canda, on accounta he kep this cuntry together by the simple fack that most Canajuns wuz unite in the feelin that they cooden stand him, even tho they kep on votin fer him, cum closist to gittin Free Traits with yer Yank. But it wuz him pull back at the last minit, feelin Briddish in his hart, tho a Yank in his pockitbook.

Them Fiftys wuz probly our gratest earer of us-U.S. co-opulation. And the steaks were hy, cuz that's wen gasolene replace otes as the mane fewl on our farm, and fer the first time us Farquharsons wuz livin like sitty peeple, eetin outside on the barbykew, and goin inside after to the bathroom. That wuz the end of yer Eatin cattlehog and the biginnin of the skweez on yer Sharm-in.

By yer Sixtys, us and U.S. wuz a 2 nayshin cartel in weet, and us farmers started to speshulize and git bigger masheens, puttin the cartel before the horse. But then Canda startid tradin with Japann and alluva suddin Precedent Linen Johnson wuz no more nice guy, and started givin sudsiddys to his weet farmers so we wooden have a chants. So Canajuns started tradin with the Serviets hopin to wipe up. The Yanks refuse to do this on relijuss grounds, Aunty-Commonism bein their Staitfaith. But we dun so blaim gud with them Bolshys, we sole them haff a bullyun dollers wortha grane. They cooden gro enuffa ther own, mostly cuz ther Stait Farm is no insurance that a fella kin care about wat he razes wen it all goes to sum sentral offiss of yer Sibble Serviss.

Now this wuz oney a yeer after that Cubist Missal Crysis

wen Khrooschev the Roosian premiere with a hole in his shoe, if not his hed, had skeered the nickers offa yer Yanks, hoo were expectin WW Three to be the nex Miami Vice. So the Yanks wuz reely pistoff at us fer tradin with ther enemas. But Ewe Ass farmers dint feel that way. They wanted to sell ther grane to hooever wud buy. This is noan as lazy-fairy or free enter-yer-prize, and their cuntry wuz founderd on it, but it tuck Canda's big trade deel with Roosia to put a rockit up Trickydick Nickson fer to go to Maw'sCow and open up Roosia fer Ewe Ass trade.

So wat did poor little nooterd Canda do? We started havin truckin trade with yer Chinee, not just yer Tie-wun-ons, but yer Big Red Mainlanders. Them Oztrailyuns got tired of bein Down and Under too, and they started bartrin ther weet up Mousey's Tung. Didden take long afore old Mousey wuz havin tee with that Sexytairy of the Staits, Henry Kissassinger, and whadda ya noe, after thirty yeer of cole war, the Staits wuz back doin wat they allwyaze dun best, sellin itself to annybuddy they met on the street.

But by swinjer it were too late. Them Jappakneesiz had got ahed of them Yanks by copycattin everythin they use to do, and now the copycats wuz topcats. On toppa that, yer Green Rezzolution, witch use to be call Point Fore or Peece Core, or Martial's Plan, or Rehabillatitillation Releef, all started to do wat they was sposed to, and endid up makin the rest of us fud perjuicers green round our gills. We had kep thinkin of Injure as a buncha hungry lil beggers in Calcutter, but mosta them Skindoos wuz out in the feelds groan sirpluss grane, and by yer end of yer 60's they wuz thurd in wirld weet produckshun. Even China got into yer ax, after they recuvverd frum the backerd effex of Mousey's Grate Leep Forerd.

Even yer thurd wirld becum hevvy exporters of the produks we had tot them to grow, but they cooden keep enny of the proffits cuz they had to pay off our bankers jist like

A hard bat agin a soft bawl.

snivelly-eyzed peeples wuz stuck doin. Now everybuddy in the wirld grows wat I grows, witch is why our guvmint wants to set me on to uther things, like gittin offa the farm and onto the pogey.

Nuther bad thing wat happen wuz yer Yerpeen Common Mark-up, to countervale all this, started pamprin its farmers with the biggest sudsidys in histry, and crematin mountins of butterfat and aigs and meet, at bargin prices, wile ther farmers clected gourmay prices.

And now the big Boogie is perteckshunism. I thot that wuz the cheef bizness of yer Mafiascos or yer Cosy Nostrils. But ever sints Briney and his Uncle Ronny has bin disgusting free traids, all we've had is the oppsit. First the Yanks open up ther shakes'n shingles bars, and hit us in our softwood lumbar regions. Then we hadda do the same thing to ther cobs to prevent them frum corn-hauling us. Now, everythin has gon to potash, with fishn hawgs waitin fer the slotter. Next up is strippin the sheets offa our steal and puttin counter veils agin our rods, pipes and tubes. Not to menshun makin our Western perjuicers hold back their gas til they've pade the price for passin it acrosst their boarders.

Seems to me that the big misteak wuz bringin up them dam 2 words Free Traid in the firsplace. We wuz gittin along jist fine with Atey purrsent no tarfs, and the Yanks, as usual, ignoring us with their undivide attenshun. But Blarney Bullroney hadda call attenshun to us wen he invit Ronny and his Nanny up to Cuebec fer that Sham Rock Consort a cuppla yeer ago.

Oh everybuddy got along jist fine. Blarney and Milly and Nanny and Runny sat round yer Shatto Fruntnacker and dropped a liddle assid rane, then Big Run tole Blarney that anytime he had a problim he shood call him on the red fone in his big White House. So Briney use to call up every weak after that, sumtimes in the middel of Big Ron's mornin, or aftnoon, or even eevenin nap. "Ron, this is Briney, " he'd say, and after bout ten minits this wood establish contack, speshully if Ragin had fergot to take his milk of amneesia. "Ron, pleese lower yer doller," Briney wood say every weak. And back wood cum the saim reply, "Well, Briney, up yers!"

But the big too-doo-doo of that weak-end in Cuebeck wuz the end of that Sham Rock Consort wen Briney got up to sing a few wurds. He had his Milly with him, at the time preggerunt with the nex liddle P.C. Jr., and Briney call Runny and Nanny fer to cum up on stage with them, on accounta it wuz Simp Hat-tricks Day, and they wuz all actin up Irish as all git out, giv er take Milly the Yougo-slobbrin.

Do you mind that nite? A lotta peeple did. We didden hav the cabel at the time, the See Bee See had our toobs all tyed up, but I seen it jist as cleer as cleer wen Briney giv his anser to Ronny Ragin on yer Free Traid. Briney open his mouth jist abuv his chin, look Ronny strait in the eye, and sung rite in his face: "And they'll stee-heel yer Arse, Away!"

Now let's be honist heer. I reely don't noe wat to think about yer Free Traids, and mebby you don't neether. The oney person I noe has a deafknit pinion on this hole thing is the wife and former sweetart. Valeeda sez that Free Traids is jist anuther cuppla fantsy wirds fer a cuppla plane wuns: Wife Swoppin. And she sez it wuzn't start up by yer Yanks

107

Yer Sham Rockers Slum It.

at all, but by yer Mets. I member them 2 pitchers use to releef eech uther on the mound then they startid releefin eech uther *offa* the mound, and by the time yer Penance wuz startin in the fall they had exchange wives, kits and the hole caboodels.

Now them free traiders kin tock all they want about wat's on or off or under yer tabel, jist like them "micky" partys we use to go to durin World War No. 2: ginger ail on the tabel, Old Overcolt on the flore. But if ther's sumthin that yer Yank is doin that Canajuns wants to git in on, like smokin the maruhjewahyena or droppin the LSD (the first assid-drane that got dropt on Canda), or that Coke that they sniff up ther noze nowadaze instedda down ther throtes with a straw: all them dis-leagel things is gonna git acrost the border past yer queer customs at Nagger Falls no matter wat we legiblate. Yuh cant make sin unpoplar, unless sum noo-fangle uncure-abull diseese happins to cum allong with it.

Thers allus bin Free Traid in idees, and foolishness and ther's no copyrite on thinkin crood thots. Fer example my boy Orville use to hav a prescripshun to that Huge Heffer maggotzeen, "Plowboy", ware all the gurls has staples in ther navels. But that don't soot Orville no more now that he's a big man and about to granulate frum the Continualation Scool and mebby git a partime job givin out gas, and pumpin air in tires. Oh no, he has to hav his "Pantyhouse". Jever see that thing? Tock about yer full frontals, goze on fer pages with everyone bear as a bird all over. But last munth's dishin wuz too mutch fer our border gards, and they rip out five pages of wat they call Orl Sects. I dunno wat that meens. Valeeda sez its 2 peeple tockin about it on the fone the day after.

Anuther noeshun that's cum acrost big frum downsouth is yer stripper. Now wate a minit. I don't meen them boomps-yer-dazy girls with the tassels in the air and the lit up brassears and the jooled jeezstrings that twinkel. That's old hats. I'm tockin about fellas paradin around to mewsick like Ravvle's "Bawly-ero", and unravvlin off ther close to a buncha screemin feemails. This is happnin rite here in Parry Sound in the luvly Goo-goo Room of our Brunsick Huttel. I ast the wife: "Valedda wood you spend yer aig munny on sumthin like that?" She snort and sed, "Heck, no, I'll jist try and ketch you cummin outa the tub sum Sardy nite."

This fella they had in lass weak wuz wun of them regler Yungstreet Strippers frum Tronto, but I betcha he start up in yer Staits and is now infilthitratin our cuntry. I spose that's wat yer Canda Counsillers calls culchural exchange. Mind you, ther's Canajun content, too. Wen this Mr. Teezy Weezy has throwed off alla his close, he stands ther jist like the day he was bored, sept fer the fack that he is warin one of Seegrim's Crown Roil bags. I cooden tell yiz wether it wuz a twenny-sixer or a micky.

As fur yer wife-swop, that happin rite heer in our own barn. The wife and I gits in the hay arselfs all thru Joon but cum Augist we genrally orgynizes a gangthrash with our nabers, wen we all mucks in together fer to git in our

109

Valeda prepares for her role in the hay.

mewchewall crops. And after the harvist is over, it's bin cus-tom-mary fer to sellibate with all them workers hoo co-opu-lated with us.

This yeer it wuz our tern. Now meself, I don't drink sept fer mebby takin a liddle cookin shairy at Chrismuss fer the wife and kidnees. But I order in six cases of Litebeer. Don't bleeve wat them ads say: that stuff is jist as hevvy as yer regler beer wen you has to carries it on yer shoalder.

Furse wun to drink up wuz old Earl Fackney, hoo is pert neer fore scores if he's a day. Well sir, after chugaluggy six or seven of them beers he start actin up like he was seven-and-teen. He jist sat ther and giggel like a ninny, never tutched a sangridge or a browny, jist kep slushin back the beer. Nex thing we noo, he up and thru his carkees in the middel of the barn flore.

Did we stop him? No. We all start actin like we wuz yung fools too and before ya noo it, all of us had throwed our kees after Erl's on the saim blaim flore, meself inclooded. Then we all doav in after them, jist a snickerin like teenyagers. Well, you kin snicker if you like, but the upshat of that hole eevnin wuz that everybuddy all end up goin home in sumbuddy elts's trackter.

But that's not yer reel end. Ther wuz 2 cupple in that barn that nite had bin in Holey Ackermoany fer ny onto twenny yeer. But that nite they both switched ther britchin. Quicker'n billy-o the wun went with the tuther, and the tuther went with the tuther's uther wun. That wuz Augist, wen they split ther long-turm britching, and I hav to tell yuh that them 2 cupples hasn't got back together yit. Nor have they excommunicait with eech uther in enny way. Havn't writ to eech uther, or tocked to eech uther even on the party line. I dout they've even *seen* ther pardners-that-wuz.

I betcha them 2 wimmin is dyin to find out how them 2 fella is gittin along cookin fer eech uther.

So mutch fer yer Free Traid.

16.
Up to Yer Arts in Culcher

ll durin them free-traid disgusting groops the
wun thing Canajuns didden wanna hav on the
table wuz enny culcher. I'm not tockin bout the
stuff that grows on cheese wen it's moldy, and I
don't meen yer agrra, or yer horta, or even yer pissy, I meen
jist strait culcher. Nobuddy here wants it on the tabel any
morn elboes, or a ketchup bottel in a hy mucky-muck
house of them peeples hoo blongs to yer Cafayteeria
Sassiety. Canajuns wants culcher under the tabel like a
Briteswine bottle at a Pressedbyteerian weddin.

I had an idee that culcher is pritty close to havin manors,
but I never bin too sure of wat it reely is. The wife sez that
culcher is wat nice peeple do after they finishes all ther wirk
and they've had ther supper. If that's the case, then culcher
is pritty much like havin a hobby.

The reezin I kinda grinds my teeth wen I heer that word is
becuz of wat them Incum Tacks peeple a few yeers back
dun to us farmers. Wether yer one of them weak-end sitty
peeples that pertends to raze a crop of grass wile wat ther
reely doin is axtendin ther big back lon to look more like a

cuntry estait, or wether yer like the wife and me hoo are jist scrapin by without much munny to show at the end of yer fizzcle yeer, then wat yer ingage in, accorn to guvmint experks, is not a bizness, but a hobby. That meens I has spent the most parta my life jist hobbyin. Ther is more hobby farmers round our parts now than ther is regler downindurty full-time toilers and swetters. I allus thot of us Farquharsons as workhorses, but terns out we is jist hobby-horses.

Lemme giv yiz a sampel of my hobby. I git up at six ayem, go strait outa a warm bed onto a cold bysickle seet fer to git back to our hardwood bush fer to git them sixteen Holsteen in frum the feeld, water 'em, feed 'em, pull 'em, strip 'em, and sweep out all ther nacheral by producks fer to add to my piles outside, so's I kin put it back to the land fer the spring re-runs. Then I feed the resta the stock, caffs, pigs, and foul mostly, bring in the aigs, then the wife waters and feeds me.

After breckfist, sints its not yit time fer the harrowin daze ahed Ile morn likley git out the old stoned bote fer to git to a far feeled and git the old rocks off. Eether that or grindin pigs ther chop, er mendin fentses, or fixin hamestraps, er givin the greesgun to old Allis Chommers er the lil Jondeer cultyvater.

But, I'm sposed to be tockin bout the uther kinda cultyvaters that tends to yer arty hobbys like paintin with oil and numbers, or Nashnul Belly dancin on yer tippy toes. I gess the point I wuz tryna make is I work sixteen our a day at my hobby wen I'm in seezon. I never noo I wuz runnin a hobby till I got a letter frum sum sibilant serpint frum yer Aggravaculcher bunch in Ottawar tellin me I had bin decalcified into a hobby, cuz I don't put out like the bigboys do. I mind the shock I felt wen I reelized that my life amount to no more than wat I dun as a boy down in our root seller, makin a moddle airyplane out a balsy wood and that funny

Dancer of yer Nashnulized Belly Cumpny.

gloo makes you git vertickle-go wen yuh sniffs it too much in a unaired basemint. It cost ten sents to buy then and it wuz jist called Dope.

Winter nites a cuppla boys on the next conseshun use to git with me and make Slopwith Camels, and Spads, frum Wirl War 1 and even them old Fokkers wat are Germin, and we'd hav a hy old time pass in the gloo around without havin the slite-ist idee why we was laffin so much. Later on wen we coodna afford any more gloo, we used to go down to the Parry Sound buss stayshun cum the weak-end, sit ther til midnite and sniff the Grayhounds.

Why cant I stick to the subjeck? Culcher. Mebby its cuz my hans get clammy wen I think of art bein everybuddy's hobby, and then fiscal fixers in Ottaway tellin me I jist bin foolin round with cows and chicks and hawgs twice a day frum sunup to sunsit. And do you noe wat reely got me in trubble with the Infernal Revenge-you peeple? Rite-in these damfool books.

Now I got no plaints agin yer pubblishurs. They treets me royalty, and they even pays me on time, giv er take sicks munths. But accorn to Seckshunal 31 of yer Canda Incum Dinkum Act, if you gits a liddle emollyment on the side, then yer farm gits put on the side as aside-line, like paintin on glass, or mackermay nittin, or even corkwirk.

So if I'm a pard-time aggerculcherist, wat duz that make me the resta the time? If I'm oney partly aggra, and I'm in the book-ritin rackit, duz that make the rest of me jist plane culcher? Duz that put me under the tabel at yer Freetraid tocks, wile the rest of me, yer hobby farmer, is splaid acrost the tabel fer all to dicker over? I tell yuh, I jist don't noe wat to put into my T-4 shorts now. Kin I express my deepreesheeayshin on my eekwipmint, or shud I jist apply fer a Canda Counsill grunt fer to go off and coutemplate my navel, and perduce anuther peesa litry fluff?

I kin tell yuh this issyuh has sure razed a tem-pist in a

115

peepot round about my parts. They say hope springs paternal and the oney hope I got is yew my deer-reeders, hopin agin hope that I'm a auther yew cant refuse. The wun thing I do noe is that hardly ennybuddy buys my books fer to reed fer therselfs. They allus push them on sum innersent relltiv at Chrismuss cuz they cant remember wat size neck they take.

Enuff about me, I bin goin on about myself as if I was a acter or a pollytishun, witch nowadaze amounts to the saim blaim thing. But I do noe well wun trooly culcherd purson and that's the wife and former sweetart, hoo wuz a regler harpyist even before I meet up with her. She serve with yer McKellar Chamber Potted Simpathy Orchester, and this yeer she is singing secund mezzaneen in our Parry Sound Sintenniel Quire, witch has an aggravation of over 60, eggsept Valeeda hoo is oney 59.

She don't harp no more, tho. After marge with me she seam fer a wile to throw up everything. She put the harp in our sepperater room, and the oney time she pulls it down now is wen she hasta cut the cheese. But she still luvs all that classified mewsick, and she drags me to consorts fer to lissen to all that catterwallin. I keep waitin fer the stuff to finely tern into a toon.

All thru our cortin daze I never miss a consort with the Parry Sound Simpathy Orkester, witch one yeer won yer Nobel Prize, with Honnerbull Menshun frum Macteer. I wuz allways in the front row admirin Valeda's pluck, and I gess lokel peeples musta took me fer a big mewsick luvver. I tell you frankly, I've luvved with it and without it; didden need no Ravvel's Ball-ee-aero fer to git me goin in them daze.

I never mutch liked the first toon they got off in every consort, till Valeeda tole me that wuz nuthin but a toon-up. I tole her sum of them instrymints cooda dun with a loob job too. Valeda sed I didden deepreesheeate wat they wuz

116

goin thru playin with eech uther. She sed Shakespeer, yer Beerd of Avon, rit "If music be the luv of food, play on!" If that's the case, then why don't rabbits sing?

The important thing fer them hi-tone orkesters is fer them all to start together and finish up the same way. I don't think anybuddy in the band cares 2 hoots what goze on in between. But that's why they have to hav a time-keeper to stand up in front and wave to beat the band. He don't hav to hav no talent, jist bring the hole rang-dang-doo in on time and under budget. In fack, I think any minnit now they'll all be replace by one of them Metrick Gnomes.

You probly think I don't noe my brass frum my hobe, but I set and watch them go thru the hole of a mewsical peece so many times that I got to like thare kinda music almost as much as ded quiet. It's sposed to be good fer yuh, accorn to the pote hoo sed it had the charms to smooth out yer savage brests.

I'll tell you yer brass frum yer uther things. They're divide up between yer strumpets, yer thrombonses, and the odd Frenched horn witch to make the blame peece of preeverted plummin work, yuh has to keep a hand in all the time. Then ther's the reedy bunch, incloodin a Anglican saxaphone er 2, and a even reedier lookin thing call a Clarion Net, and a buncha floots looks like horse's thurmommeters.

Back in the back so's they cant make too much noize is wat they call yer timp-knees. That's ware they set ther snares, get ther kettles reddy and wait fer hours to git a lit-tle bang on yer infernal tryangle. The big noise is got up by yer fiddles. You never herd sitch a catter-wallin wen they all scrapes and bows together. They cums in three sizes, first the regler old-time fiddles that everybuddy chucks under ther chins, soopervize by the foreman to the conducker, called yer fiddlehed. The large famly size fiddel is the bull of the famly, a big stand-up sucker looks like a up-ended punt.

117

This is yer hevvy draft fiddel. In the middel, ther's the kind you have to go squatty-roo fer to play. I fergit wat theez ones is called, and the wife is out strainin her creem so I ast Orville, the boy wunder, and he tole me they wuz called after wat we jist had fer dessert...Jello!

Then there's yer woods with wind, witch incloods yer hoboe, a ill wind that nobuddy blows gud, and the bigger rig that wen you play it looks like yer burpin a bedpost. Orville don't noe the name of that eether, fer he called it a bassoon, witch as everybuddy noes is one of them munkys with a red and bloo bottom. But wen they all plays together they kin go like a 4-horse team over a log bridch in a cloud of horseshat and small stones. It all cums out smooth as a barl of pig chop, but it's nuthin ya kin dance to.

You take yer good square dants toon, like "Munny Musk" or "Chikken in the Bedpan, Chikken in the Haul" or "You Turkeys in the Straw", now that's got a good thump to her, lotsa jinicker, and with a reel whang to her, you cood keep on dansin only to the drum. Now that's wat I call cultyvatin eech uther, cuz you gits to dance with everybuddy on the flore as you dosey dose and granchange with all the men left.

'Taint like that bawlsroom dansin in the sitty ware you oney trots with wun person at a time. On the slow stuff, it jist looks like neckin standin up and yu'd be better off in the back of a Bewick. As fer the yung tads, and ther froogin rottin-roll dantsin, that don't make no sents atall. They don't hardly moove ther feats, jist ther abominabull mussels. They don't tutch eech uther, don't tock to eech uther, don't eeven look at eech uther. My gol, you think them teenyfloppers had bin merried to eech uther fer thirty-five yeer!

Wun thing yer guvmint culcher vulchers is big on is fer to keep yer Canajun Content, and they dont meen makin us awl as heppy as piggs in shoos. We never thunk about this

thurty yeer ago wen our toobs wuz tyed to jist the wun
Chanel, Nummer Five, and we used to watch Don's Messy
Ilanders, with Marg 'n Charly doin a ellfunt stomp jist afore
they rippt into yer weakly Godsong. Then ther wuz everybuddy's Sweethart Shurly Harmher, the girl frum Hornys
Corners, folleyed by Boob Ghoul-eh, folleyed by yer Hip
Prade with Joist Hun and Wall-ey Coster, folleyed by yer
comix Wain in Shoestore. Now all we got left is Tommy
Humper, without them Alien Sisters. I miss Corally and
Anually, or Mick Mack and Jerk, yer Rithm Pills. Thank
god fer Al Churnme, hoo still makes all them sweet sounds
wile he's on the fidel draggin the tale of a horse crost the
guts of a cat.

Valeda sez all that ain't culcher, jist recremational fun.
Her idee of reel culcher is lissenin to sumthin like Lone
Grin. I tole her I bin lissenin to him ever sints he dun the
noos durin the war makin Canda Carry On with the Voice of
Gloom, till he cross-over to the Staits and becum father of
ther cuntry on that Poundaroaster Ranch, and end up sellin
dogfud, witch maid me stay away frum them Poundaroaster
Restrunts.

But she's not talkin' bout the denouncer with a voice like
a bumblebee in a jug; she meens yer Grand Ole Opry, the
wun that is writ by ded peeple not from Mashvill, but frum
over ther in Yerp ware all the forners cums from. Jermin
peeple like Ritchcard Waggoner, the immoral de-composer
of Opry. Valeeda sez the word is immortle, meenin it goze
on and on ferever. Valeeda cood sit ther all afternoon in
front of the raddio and lissen to his hole Godderdammerung
thing. Wen it cums to that kinda culcher, the wife is a regler
Ringwurm.

This spring she bussed herself down to Tronto fer to heer
that hy-risin tenner, Plassid Flamingo, cuvver a lot of arias
all by hisself. And she wuz offal disappoint that this Span-
ish fly all the way over here and hadda sing in Harld Bal-

lard's icy play-pen, yer Make Beleev Gardens, cuz Tronto aint classy enuff to have no Opry House. Even Norse Bay, Gateway to Parry Sound, has a noo culcher senter that Plaster Dummingo cooda sung in. But Valeda sed she sat in yer Greys and close her eyes and let her eers fill up with all that singin, and by doin that it was jist as good as bein back home lissenin to the stars of yer Metrapopolitan and uther Insurience cumpnys singin fer Texassco on the raddio.

To me all that yellin sounds like a buncha tomcats makin out on a tin ruff in a halestorm and givs me nuthin but a pain, but Valeeda sez that's the hole idee. It's the same as yer sope opry, sepp them singers gives it to yuh at the topp of ther lungs, full throatle. They throatles therselfs so much yuh cant make out a blaim thing they're tryna sing, but Valeeda sez they're in as much pane as us lissenin. All them deep bartones and fancy divas and small-mouth bassos don't jist sing wen they're happy. They sing even more wen they're ornery, speshully wen they're dyin fit to bust.

You take that La Traviesty by Joe Green. (Valeeda minds his Eyetalian name but I sure don't.) It's bout Violenta, hoo is one of them Paris street bizzybodys no bettern she shood be, hoo gits dizeezed with yer gallopin consumpshun. Duz she take to her bed and sneek under the cuvvers with a bottla Tryminmycal DM? Not fir bobnuts, nosirree. She's out ther by the fitlites with her deep throte beltin out the hy-notes and breethin hard till the last kickoff.

Well sir, if that's culcher it don't sound to me like Canajun culcher and that's the stuff we're sposed to take regler. P.R. Berton and Furry Mowit clames if they don't git a good dose of it every day they both gits nerviss as cut cats. It's sposed to look after wat they calls our eyedensity crysis. Meself I wooda gon to see a good optimist about that sorta thing.

I think farmin is havin the eyedensity Crysis that culcher has bin tockin about. It's eezy to fergit hoo yuh are wen the guvmint tells yuh yer not a farmer no more, but jist a part-time nuthin'. To me reel culcher is the gloo that binds us all togither in the saim commune-a-titty wether it's a town, a township or a hole country. Culcher is the slum tote-all of all of us and the reesin we is happy fer to stick together. That's stronger than guvmint bonds and morn a museeum cleckshun of secund-hand relicks and anteeks.

The place I grode up in had all of the things that made us

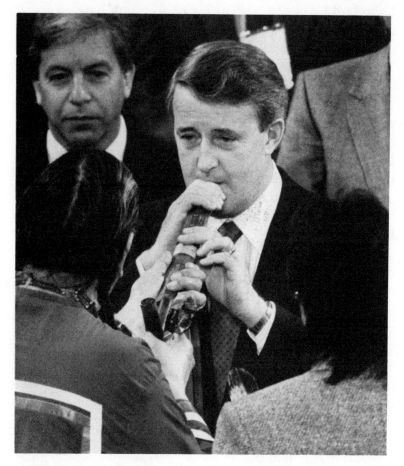

Briney Bullrooney makes a toke-in jestyer to yer aboriginal inhibitants.

want to be part of eech uther, and we got the prufe of it this yeer wen Parry Sound had its Sintennyell and all them Baby Bloomers that had excaped to the sitty, cum back fer a weak er two and reminded therselfs that they had cum frum sumwares deafknit, that alluva sudden ment more to them than any noo place they went to. They felt this way morn sum of us hoo staid. This is mebby happnin to morn more peeple as ther lifes work starts to dry up and ther bein forsibly retard before ther time. That's wen yuh looze yer reel culcher, it's like takinyer sole frum yer bawdy, wen they uproutes yuh like a weed without no pratickle meens of keepin yerself together.

Briney Bullroomy cum into his offiss shoutin "Jobs, jobs, jobs!" He musta ment morn sentaurs, sexretarys, embarsadores and paper-hangers and painters at 24 Sucksex Drive. I cud see every pogey purson in Canda cleenin up our environly-mint wile the employables is bizzy dirtyin it up. We cleen up our parks after our Dumb Minion day binj so why don't we do it with our rivers and laiks? This kinda hy culcher cood be the biggest groath industry on our tooryist agender.

But Valeeda sez that's jist housework outside, not reel culcher. So she drug me down to that Shakespeer Festeral one day last fall wen it wuz too wet fer her to plow. We lookt it up on the map and ther it wuz among all them vary-close vanes of hi-ways, Shakespeer, Ontario.

Shakespeer, Ontario is a servissable station, a cheez shop, a buncha garden ormyments flutterin in the breeze and no Festerall at all. We got outa town in twenny secunts and ast a fella hoein his termips: "Wher's yer Shakespeer Festeral?"

"Ate mile down the rode in Stratfurd!"

"Wat in the Sam Hell is the Shakespeer festerall doin in Stratford?"

"Don't ast me. They bin callin it that fer 35 yeer now and
122

they've never got anybuddy frum Shakespeer fer to go the ate mile all the way in to see the fool thing."

I wuz reddy to tern back, but Valeeda sed we had cum all that way fer Canajun culcher, and by swinjer we wuz gonna git it both barls. We had a choist atween a sityation comedy call "Luv's Lost Wen yer in Laber" and a sityation trajiddy call "Mac and Beth". Valeeda figgerd we hadden cum all this way fer to fool around, so we went fer the seeriuss bizness.

I'm sorry now we spent the munny. Tern out to be a merder play and we left after the first emissyun cuz we gessed long afore that hoo had dunnit. I'll tell ya one thing, it wernt the butler—he were too drunk. I ast Valeeda if she'd druther hav gone to yer Shaw Festeral down by yer Naggers-on-the-Lake. Valeda sed that hole thing wuz a fake too on accounta the Shaw wuz ded and the place had bin tuck over by yer Ayetoleyuh Cockamamie. Valeda sez she bets yer late Shaw's wife the Shan had a fit wen that happen. I'm glad we wuzn't around wen the fit hit the Shan.

17.

On yer Nees

These days a lotta uppity class peeple preefurs culcher to relijun. They think if they gose to sum hy mucky-muck deep consert or watch peeple take off ther parts at a play or even a Caddme-reward-winnin moovy, that they are doin therselfs as much good as if they went to cherch and fell asleep.

I got one of them in our own home. He's not yet a big sitty dood but he sure is lookin to be, and fer a start our boy Orville is one of them Aithywists, if he noo wat it ment. Fer sertin he's at leest a Agnostickletick. Orville wooden noe wat sich big words is all about. He jist thinks he is modren and I am a anteek, past tents.

On Sundys he hangs out in his bedroom a-twangin on his fender-bender geetar and sez wat's the use of goin to cherch wen the hole wirld has gon to helena handcart and has bin doin' it fer thousands of yeers. I tole him: "Orville, water has bin around fer millyuns and millyuns of yeers, so there's sumthin you kin do about the stait of yer neck!"

Fer all of his tock about a hancart on the way to Hell, Orville don't reely bleeve ther is sich a place. I tole him

124

takin a good look round his bedroom wood giv him a pritty good sampel. But he noes fer sertin that there's no sutch thing as the devvil. He's got it all figger out, jist like wen he found out about the Tuth Faery and yer Eesterbunny and Sandy Claws. Orville sez it's the same with the Devvil, he's reely yer old man.

I wunder sumtimes hoose side the devvil is on wen I hear about all the sandals mung them TV vangelists. I feel kind of embarse as a hammerchewer cricketsizing these relijuss perfessionals but sumthin has gon askrew. I mind wen we first got the cabel fer the TV that Valeeda cud hardly tare herself away frum them preechers on the lil box fer to git arselfs to cherch on time. Ferst to reely catch her eye was yer Orl Rubberts, hoo tole everybuddy to put ther hands on toppa the TV set wile he heeled them. Valeda dun it and she clames it dun her arthuritis a lotta good. The cat use to do the same after givin berth, and it seem to help her too. So I figgerd ole Oral cood help me with my problem, and sittin on the set did seem to help my hemmeroids. Only problem wuz it wuz hard fer Valeda and the cat to watch the show. Our TV repareman sez it wuz probly the ultry-violents in them Cat-Hoad Ray Toobs that wuz doin the good works.

Ernst Angely wuz the one seem to make heeling into a contack sport. Corse yuh hadda be ther fer to git the benny-fit of his layin on of hands. And cood he ever lay them on, tho. Use to giv yer sicken yer halten yer laim a good smack with the back of his hand rite acrost ther foreheds. I think the reeson he wore his toopee down so close to his brows is so nobuddy cood take it into ther heds fer to giv him a good crack back. But he dun good tho'. I seen him morn wunce git rid of sumbuddy's deffness by a good whack acrost the forehed. Valeda allows it wuz a mirrorkill, and I ain't gonna go agin that. Mind you, them smart blows to the hed cooda nock sum of the wacks outa ther eers.

Then sum of them Godly peeple started fer to git into pollyticks. First off, they got into the primer marys, reckomendin sertin candied-daits hoo wuz wat they cald part of yer Morl Minorrity. Yuh wuz eether on there Hit Prade or ther Hate Prade, and by gollys back in '84, this kind of hevvinly interfeerents seem to work. Now, one of ther nummers, Pat Robbertson, is aimin to go frum yer pullpit to yer bullpit by runnin fer Precedent. He dun this, he sez, after he tocked a hooravacane out of cummin near yer Eestcoast. My gol, if he kin dicktate the wether he'll sure be a shoo-in with farmers.

Last few yeers all them fellas, Billy Grame (hoos still a crackerjack), Rex Humbug, Ernst Angellee, Jimmy Swaggerer, and Jerry Foulwell, has dun a lotta tockin about how important it is to git born agin. They don't hav to tell me that. Land has to be born agin jist as much as peeple. The syckle of berth, deth and rezzumreckshun is in fronta me every day of the year. Nuthin that dyes in naycher is ded fer too long. It gits change by yer Muther's naycher into sum uther life form.

Oney critter that trys to void this sykle of renooal with yer Muther Erth is yuman beans hoo buys therselfs big mettle caskits fer to git a garnteed lay-away plan that is seepproof fer to giv them a copper-bottomed Eterminal rest. Seems like they don't want to be born agin like the resta yer vegibble and aminal kingdums.

But I don't think that's wat the laidest TV preechers is tockin about. They're tryna bring Hevvin back on erth but, as it has terned out, mostly fer therselfs. Wen Valeda furst lade site of yer Pity Hell Club, she thot that Leevit to yer Beever had teem up with yer Flyin Nun. It seam to be on all ours of the day er nite, witch ment I spose that Jimm 'n Tammy Fay was constantly havin the re-runs.

Valeda dint care wether they wuz Pennycosters or Fuddlementalists, she jist felt rite at home with them. It wuz like watchin yer Jolly Carson show combine with yer Weel

P.T.L.: Pope Try Lower.

of Farchune, and yet all the munny wuz goin to God. Ther dint seem to be no serm-ins, jist a lotta fun-razing.

Ther wernt no commershuls on the show, mostly becuz, to me, the hole show seem like 1 long commershul. Wen they wuzn't tellin yuh how the Gud Lord kin bring yuh everythin yuh want, they wuz eggstractin pennies frum widders and orfins to put ther mites in regler as crockwork jist like yer installedment plan.

If they bleeved God cood bring yuh anythin, how cum they always pitched us fer things wen it cum to munny? Even Orl Rubberts up in his Prairtower cooden seem to git his blessins strait frum the Big Deposseter in the Sky. In fack, he sez, God put the arm on him and held him with a pritty strick dedline too. I jist cant imajin Our Lord holdin anybody fer ransid like that.

Neerer my gold to thee.

But wat peeple giv Jimm 'n Tammy shure showed up on ther show, buy and buy. Fer they bilt a kind of Holey Dizzlyland call His'n Hertage U.S.A. It look like yer averedge K-mart shopper's idee of Hevvin on Erth, incloodin' a big long water-ride bilt speshully fer backsliders. Not too long ago, it cum about that the oney reel ride wuz the ones them penshunners and uther doners wuz gittin frum Jim 'n Tammy.

Wen it furst cum out that Tammy had gon to yer Beddy-fored Clink, Valeda figgerd she musta bin sufferin frum terminal eye shadder. Terns out it was oney over-yer-counter drug dickshun. I dunno wat she wuz on, but both hern her huz-bin has bin sufferin the bufferin of the Faits ever sints.

Valeda refuse to bleev all that stuff about adulthood and them fairy storys about homeo-seckshunality. Jim had sed his back wuz to the wall the hole time and that wuz gud enuff fer the wife, both his and mine.

I think it was wen Valeda saw a little auction on the TV of

sum of Jimm 'n Tammy's things that she got offa her nees and open her eyes. Everything was bein renderd up to Seezure fer to raze the munny that was missin frum the Prayer peeple's books. The minster that tuck over tempuarily, Richer Dork, fess up that sum of the munny went fer to blackenmale that cherch sexretary hoo wuz takin dick-tayshun from Jim. But the rest wuz so far gon it cooda bin in yer Barenooda Eterminal Tryangle.

But the stuff them 2 had clected wile on ther daly missyuns of mersy! Tammy even had a shamdeleer in her clozzit, and it maid yuh wonder how she ever got a chanst to play it. Mebby Jim did, cuz he wuz relucktint fer to cum outa the closet. I bet ther sorry they lost that air-condishun doghouse. They cood probly use it fer to liv in wen they gits bounced from Pamsprings.

The pollytishuns dint let us down in yer sandals department, neether, witch sure cozzed Gary's Hartbrake. Seems to me that the watchwerd of our lait aities is to take yer Ten Commandmints and put after them, wat my boy Orville reeds on his exam papers: "Candied-dates shood not attemp more than three of thees."

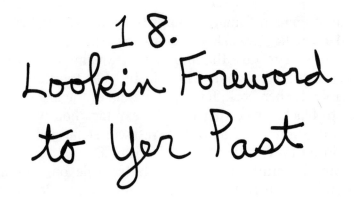

18.
Lookin Foreword
to Yer Past

The golf club has calld back agin. They want all of our farm sept the homested and outbildins and the barnyard, and the fallofeeld next to it. That's about five or sex akers. Don't ast me wat the hectares it cums to.

Valeda and I jist had a slumit confluents. She sez we kin tern most of them 5 akers into a garden and liv off it and the chicken house and the strippins frum mebby fore cow and the odd hawg. The vegibles we kin sell fresh all summer to them hy-mucky-muck tooryists frum the States that cums to them big summer huttels in Muskoky like yer Windersmear, yer Brit Ania and yer Big 1 Inn.

I tole the wife and former sweetart to go out and take down that "Fur Sail" sine. If Canda is about to becum a toorst trap then we is gonna be part of the bait. Ile git into town and buy the wife and me a cuppla them Jackie Cooper plastical hocky hellmits. At leest if we drops ded in our trax it'll be on our own land.

Oney thing worrys me about this becummin tooryist operaiters, and ternin Canda into yer Last Resort, is our

130

reppitayshun fer bein so nice in the manors departmint. All over the wirld we is infamous fer bein so nice. I wanna tell yuh I ain't seen it round these parts, speshully frum yer yunger ginration. Orville wooden noe "pleesinthankyew" if he fell over them.

The uther day I wuz trundlin the wife's aigs around muskokey wen I wuz stop on the hi-way by sum yung buck hoo force me over to the side of the rode and maid me git outa the car. I thot he musta bin a robber, but he claim he wuz a pleeceman. Wernt dress like the boyzen bloo that I noe frum yer Oh Pee Pees. He had a brown cote, black pants with a yella stripe down the side. I figgerd he had a cold. And on his sholders wuz the inishuls R.C.M.P. I noo he wuzn't one of our Musical Riders cuz he didden hav no Boy Scout hat and the cheery red sportscote, so I figgerd him fer one of them Roman Cathlick Members of Parlmint. He musta bin collectin funds fer the seppertist scools, cuz he tride to fine me fifty doller fer goin thirty killergrams over the spede limmit down the middel of a 2 lane hi-way. I brung out my drivers liesints.

"You must be sum forner," I sed. "We're aloud to do both them things in Ontaryo." And I showed him ware it sed at the bottom of that liesints "Tare Along the Dotted Line".

Now mebby that ain't so much bad manors as iggerunce, but that saim day I wuz giv the wirst outbirst of it I ever seen. I had bin to Bo Morris and Brit Ania huttels, and still had sum aigs left, so I wuz lookin fer the last huttel on my list wen I got lost. Eezy to do up in Muskokey, lemme tell yuh.

Now Canajuns is noan all over the wirld as plite peeple. Dull as ditchwater, they may say, but plite. But my boy Orville's contempyouairys don't seam to have any of the swave fine-ass akwire by his elders. Lemme tell yuh wat happin.

131

It wuz gittin on fer dusk, and no gaz stations around fer to ask the way. Nuthin but trees, rox and bush. That wuz the time I cooda use the servasses of one of yer R.C.'s M.P., but them suckers is never around wen you wanna ask fer direckshun.

The oney kinda habitatayshun I seen wuz a liddle car parked in sum bushes off a county rode. I druv up behind, put my brites on, and wated fer them wuz in the car to cum out and give me a assissed. Ther wuz a cupple in the backseet but they never maid no moove. Leest they never maid no mooves to git outa the car, ther seem to be plenty of fustlin and rustlin goin on inside. So I finely got outa my pickup and cum over and looked in the reer windy. I cooden see the face of the fella but the girl wuz fazin me direck and lookin at me offal upset and red in the face. I rap on the reer windy and sed, "Roll down yer winder!" That maid the fella finely tern around and both him and the gurl together yell: "Up Yores!"

Well, I cooden see the sents of goin back to my truck jist fer to raze the winda. So I kep rappin. Finely I figgerd I'd git both of ther divideed attenshun if I yell a kwestyun thru the glass loud enuff. I dun that and I wuz anserd back with the most offal barge of vitooperative profannititty that I have ever herd. And all I said to this yung cupple wuz: "How far is yer Big One Inn?"

Now you can call me a rinkle ole prood, a relick of a throwback stuck in the gumboo fer fifty yeers; I don't keer. That looks like my fewcher frum now on: goin back to my primeevil ruts the way I started. I'm gonna be a happy hoer in my 5-aker patch, and I don't have to be a man outstandin in his feeld, cuz I'll be close enuff to get back to the house without goin agin the grane. I'm gonna be livin like my incesters wen they first start up this plaice morn a hunnert yeer ago, and it don't bother me, nossir.

I've see the past and it werks.

Eppylog

Our garden will keep us bizzy the munths of Joon, Jooly and Awgist. So shood I jist jestait fer the uther 9 munth of the yeer? We oney go south once evry winter; last yeer we got as far as Orillyuh.

Tell you the trooth, I'm thinkin of runnin next fall. I'm not tockin about jogglin, I'm tockin bout Parlmint. Them fellas gits a reesess fer three hole munths if they duz ther work rite the rest of the yeer, so it won't intyfear with our 5 aker garden. Frum wat I heer mosta them M.P. suckers terns up fer oney 1 hour a day fer the Questing Peeriod, then goes to a doller forty-nine sent sex-corse dinner in the Parlmentally Restrunt, and probly spends the resta the day ritin letters home on accounta the free postedge. Well, it's bettern bein on pogey. In fack it's jist like bein on pogey, oney goin fursclass.

Valeda thinks if I try sich a thing I'll likely fall off my stump, and blow my deeposset. I probly wood if I thru my hat in the ring of any of the oldtime partys. But wat about them oddballs bunches beyond yer frinch? Like the

133

Me, Charlie Farquharson, up the stump.

Ryenose-sasserasses hoo cum out of the woodswork and try to horn in every fore yeer. They had them kinda crazees in the Anglish lection this yeer, yer Ravin Monster Loony Party, and yer Lets Hav Anuther Party Party hoos members cood hardly stand on ther platforms without fallin off.

The trubble with all them kinds of partys is they thinks the way to get lected is to do sumthin reely foolish fer to git peeple's attenshun. Ackshully with yer Grits and yer Endeepees and yer Regressive Preservativs, it's jist the uther way round. Them birds gets therselfs lected first, and then start actin foolish.

I'm gonna git a party of my own, the F.U. party (Farmers Unite, of coarse), and yer all invited, Fall of '88. I dunno hooze fall it's gonna be but Valeda sez if it's mine I mite as well go for broke. Heck, I tole her, I'm there now! But she dont want me to settel for no back debenches, or even yer Cabnuts.

I figger ther's bound to be a minorty guvmint no matter hoo gits in and then everbuddy'll be lookin to shack up together like Daisy Peterson dun with that D.P. Boob Rae amung yer Queens Porkers in Ontaryo.

If Canajuns is lookin fer a reel opprest minorty yuh cant beet yer small farmers. Now that I am consider to be useless and out of it, I aim to be Prime Minister. I promiss not to move more furncher into 24 SusSex Drive. In fack, we may even hav a littel auction, so if yer lookin fer sich a thing, exersixe yer french-frize fer Charlie. It's time we had a reel common man in yer Common House.

F.U. in '88.

THE END
(Mebby not!)
135

Photo Credits

Page 5: Canapress; page 7: *Toronto Star*; page 14: *Maclean's* Photo Library; page 18: *Maclean's* Photo Library; page 25: Canadian Pacific Railway; page 29: *Toronto Star*; page 32: *Globe and Mail*; page 45: Canapress; page 48: Canapress; page 53: Canapress; page 56: *Financial Post*/ David Burcsik; page 64: Information Canada; page 71: Canapress; page 72: Canapress; page 75: Canadian Armed Forces; page 77: *Financial Times*/ Hugh Rutledge; page 83: *Globe and Mail*; page 89: Canapress; page 92: Canapress; page 93: Canapress; page 98: Canapress; page 101: Canapress; page 103: Canapress; page 106: Canapress; page 108: Canapress; page 114: Canapress; page 121: Canapress; page 127: Canapress; page 128: Canapress; page 134: Joan Nicholls.

All photos used with permission.